Advance Praise for *Shimmering Images*
by Lisa Dale Norton

"*Shimmering Images* is a practical, simple, and wonderfully concise guide for memoirists seeking to improve their craft as well as those who are just getting started."
—Debra Ginsberg, author of *Waiting, Raising Blaze,*
About My Sisters, and *Blind Submission*

"Lisa Norton reminds us in this wonderfully wise and accessible book that the act of storytelling is mythmaking, and writing memoir is storytelling; whatever myth you sculpt from your past will influence your future. This helpful book itself is perfectly sculpted: The writing tools Norton expertly shares enable us to bring into brilliant clarity the defining moments in our lives. Norton convinces us that writing memoir, the sheer act of sharing your truth, can not only transform your life, but can transform the world. If you are writing a memoir, you must read *Shimmering Images*."
—Page Lambert, author of *In Search of Kinship* and leader of River
Writing Journeys for Women and Outdoor Writing Adventures

"You can read this book in an hour—but the impact could well last a lifetime. It's simple, smart, and inspiring."
—Jennie Nash, author of *The Last Beach Bungalow*

"*Shimmering Images* is an encouraging, smart, and surprisingly funny guide, full of well-tested exercises and approaches. Lisa Dale Norton teaches memoir writers how to get beyond blame and self-pity, how to find the compassion that leads to new insights, how to be 'bone honest' with themselves. She is a very wise coach who understands that the writing process is the way to truth, and that truth is complex and deep. This 'handy little guide' will transform the lives of those who need to understand their pasts in order to change their futures—that is to say, all of us. Trust me, she says: And we do, we do."

—Meg Files, author of *Meridian 144, Home Is the Hunter,* and *Write from Life,* and director of the Pima Writers' Workshop

"This book shimmers with thought-provoking insights and truth, and Lisa Dale Norton's elegantly spare formula is a valuable addition to the literature on the topic. Even though she specifically addresses only the memoir form, her system of memory retrieval and organization will be useful to any life writer."

—Sharon M. Lippincott, author of *The Heart and Craft of Lifestory Writing*

"Lisa Dale Norton's practical and lively guide to writing memoir is like having your very own writing coach holding your hand and guiding you through your story with patience and humor. Her clear, good advice covers everything you'll need to start writing: the difference between memoir and autobiography, claiming your own voice, finding the heart of your story, and finally crafting it into a piece of work to send out into the world."

—Barbara Abercrombie, author of *Courage and Craft* and *Writing Out the Storm*

"Like a smart friend in whom you can confide, Lisa Dale Norton leads you not only through the issues of craft you'll need in order to form your life stories into art, but—perhaps more important—through the emotional landscape such work requires. A thoughtful, helpful tool for anyone facing the challenge of memoir."

—Samantha Dunn, author of *Faith in Carlos Gomez*

" 'Shimmering Images' is how Lisa Norton describes those flashes of memory that haunt us on the brightest of days or in the darkest of tunnels when least expected. Indeed they are fleeting moments in time we cannot forget because we responded emotionally and our lives were forever changed. Moved to great heights of joy, we want to share our feelings with the world. Scarred by fear, anger, or loss, we want to dig deeper and recapture and share the hope and love that healed. Memoirists feel compelled to take this journey, and in her book Lisa Norton provides a map to show us where to begin, which way to turn, and, most important, how to dig up and unlock the truths that were always there, waiting to be told. Anyone who has ever wanted to write memoir needs this precious little handbook to find out where and how to start, and, better still, how to keep going in the right direction."

—Penny Porter, author of *Heartstrings and Tail-Tuggers* and *Adobe Secrets,* and a former president and membership chair of the Society of Southwestern Authors

"*Shimmering Images* is the quintessential book on memoir writing and should be required reading for anyone who is thinking about crafting a memoir."

—Jennifer McCord, a former president of the Pacific Northwest Writers Association

"Lisa Dale Norton's little book is a bighearted treasure. She gives writers specific guidance, her voice one of passionate encouragement. Norton's message is that when getting going on a memoir, process means more than product—only through a disciplined and creative process can a writer experience the hard-won satisfaction that leads to a book. This spirited guide will be a deskside companion to memoirists old and new for years to come."

—Thomas Larson, author of *The Memoir and the Memoirist*

"In *Shimmering Images*, Lisa Dale Norton gently takes you by the hand and leads you through the process of getting down the story of your life. You learn how to access your Shimmering Images—the people, places, and events that are the source of your most powerful stories. You discover how to connect these images to the key turning points in your personal journey, and weave them into the rich tapestry that is your life. Practical and inspiring, *Shimmering Images* is a must-have for anyone contemplating writing a memoir."

—Carol Franco, coauthor of *The Legacy Guide*

"In *Shimmering Images* Lisa Dale Norton traces a clear stimulating path to writing a memoir. Norton starts with the ideas behind the process, how story transforms experience on the page. She then gives the step-by-step process that she has been teaching for decades—finding Shimmering Images (memory pictures) and weaving them into a whole. In the third part Norton looks at some of the tools to craft the process. In writing bighearted, compassionate stories, we contribute to changing the world. Norton's book is bighearted and compassionate. It is a gift to the reader."

—Susan M. Tiberghien, author of *One Year to a Writing Life*

"*Shimmering Images* has what it takes to be an outstanding how-to book for aspiring writers. It is sound, fertile, imaginative; it guides the aspiring writer around the pitfalls and into the delights of turning memories into memoir. It inspires and grounds the writer with a combination of practical, easy-to-follow steps, a rationale for engaging in this challenging process in the first place, and ways to sustain the effort for the long haul. I would recommend this book to teachers as well as to adults who are working on this genre individually."

—Muriel Dance, Ph.D., director of the Center for Continuing Education, Antioch University Seattle

"*Shimmering Images* is a marvelously uncomplicated little book. Read it through once for the gorgeous sentences, but on the second run, get to work! With Lisa Dale Norton's kind guidance, you'll have your life shimmering on paper in no time, a universe to give to friends or family or even the whole wide world."

—Bill Roorbach, author of *Writing Life Stories*

Shimmering Images

ALSO BY LISA DALE NORTON

Hawk Flies Above:
Journey to the Heart of the Sandhills

Shimmering Images

A HANDY LITTLE GUIDE

TO WRITING MEMOIR

Lisa Dale Norton

ST. MARTIN'S GRIFFIN

NEW YORK

www.stmartins.com

Library of Congress Cataloging-in-Publication Data

Norton, Lisa Dale.
    Shimmering images : a handy little guide to writing memoir / Lisa Dale Norton.—1st ed.
        p. cm.
    ISBN-13: 978-0-312-38292-6
    ISBN-10: 0-312-38292-8
    1. Biography as a literary form—Study and teaching.   I. Title.

CT22 .N67 2008
808'.06692—dc22

                                                            2008012466

First Edition: August 2008

10 9 8 7 6 5 4 3 2 1

For my mother, Nancy Sayre Somermeyer,
who taught me about beauty
and the virtues of simple language

CONTENTS

Contents

ACKNOWLEDGMENTS

I thank Hubert Wuerzner for his sweet love and support as I made a new life in Santa Fe and rewrote *Shimmering Images*, yet again.

Deep gratitude goes to my mother, Nancy Sayre Somermeyer, and my brother, William Hayden Norton, Jr., for their love and support through all the seasons our family has known, and to my father, William Hayden Norton, who taught me how to dream, and who supports me even now from beyond the veil.

Gene Dieken has *always* been there for me, and it has meant the world to me.

Karli June Hansen has offered years of deep understanding, evocative ideas, and silly playfulness that have invigorated my creativity.

Georganne O'Connor has helped me remember the daily pleasures of life and has shared a passion for ideas and a commitment to words.

Ann Cerny and I grew up together on the Ridge in Osceola. She has walked with me through the toughest of times. I bless her loyalty and the bonds of history.

Kathy Hanson's friendship has kept me on track as I worked to maintain my writing career.

I am grateful to Norma Seely for her lifelong pursuit of stories and the writing life, and the kinship we have shared on that path.

Dave Gillis offered critical support during a difficult transition in my life. I will always remember his guidance, which kept me on track as a writer.

Elizabeth Lyon, longtime friend and colleague, advised and guided me during the writing of *Shimmering Images*. I credit her for helping manifest its final form.

Hannelore Hahn, founder and director of the International Women's Writing Guild, has been a supporter for over twenty years, and I thank her for the many opportunities she has given me to develop the ideas in this book.

I am indebted to George Witte, editor in chief at St. Martin's Press, for his support over the years and for his enthusiastic response to *Shimmering Images*.

My literary agent, Elizabeth Wales, stepped in and shepherded this book, offering astute advice and moral support.

Daniela Rapp, my editor, wisely guided this project, and I am grateful to the whole team at St. Martin's, especially production editor Julie Gutin, copyeditor Barbara Wild, cover designer Elizabeth Connor, page designer Maggie Goodman, proofreaders Miranda Ford and Christina MacDonald, and publicist Ellis F. Trevor.

In the end, my deepest thanks circle back to a place called The Big Six Country Club and the two people who in 1960 risked the foolish and undoable, and set out on a journey that would make that place and that land central to my soul. In so doing they not only created a home for my heart, but they showed me the wisdom of leaping even when you can't see the ground.

FOREWORD

Over the past few years memoir has enjoyed an upsurge in popularity, and that's really good news. Clearly, there is something exciting and important about the very personal process of writing our stories and sharing them with others. Some might call it self-indulgent, or even narcissistic, to become so wrapped up in our own lives. But for the serious memoirist, the act of writing is much more than that. I think of the writings of Anaïs Nin, whose "diaries," as she called them, were not only elegantly written but took readers deep into the inner mysteries of her life. Some of what she wrote was painfully intimate, reminding us of the closeness we all long for. And often it was this intimacy that universalized Anaïs's most personal and even embarrassing scenes.

Lisa Dale Norton, like Anaïs Nin, discovered the potential power of the memoir as an art form. Anaïs once said that memoirists live not just one life but two, explaining that "there is the living and then there is the writing. There is the second tasting, the delayed reaction." This may very well describe why we write memoir, for it is often in the delayed reaction, long after the actual living, that we can fully savor the fruits of our experience.

It is important, I think, to remember that memoir—the sharing of the stories of our lives—was the source of great wisdom in ancient times. For tens of thousands of years storytelling circles provided the magic of telling others about our own experiences, and in this way we literally built bridges between our consciousnesses. The stories we tell each other not only entertain but allow us to see that we are not, after all, alone. This is how we create the mysterious bonds that connect us as couples, as lovers, as friends, as family members, and as participants in a community or a nation.

Our stories are important, for it is through them that we discover our humanness and the universality of our personal lives. Some years ago, when I was teaching a seminar in northern California, I asked my class to write a story that was particularly close to the bone. I explained that I wanted them to write about experiences that had changed their lives. As they got out their pens and paper, I noticed that one woman, sitting in the back of the class, began to weep. I was willing to bet that she would not be one of the people who volunteered to read to us what she had written. But I was very wrong. She was the first to volunteer.

She stood up, holding the small, leather-bound journal where she had written her assignment. Her hands shook and even before she started reading tears were flowing down her cheeks. The story she told was filled with horror. She had been in a crowd at a university, where she had just matriculated, when someone with a high-powered rifle began shooting. Several people were killed and numerous others were badly wounded. My student had escaped physical injury but not the wounds inflicted that day on her soul. After reading her story she looked around the hushed room and told us that she had never before shared this experience with anyone. She had held it in for more than twenty years. She saw the tears in the eyes of her classmates as she closed her journal and turned to take her seat. And then, tearfully, she apologized for upsetting everyone by telling her story.

Instantly, an older woman stood up and in a passionate voice thanked the storyteller for her courage in the reading. She then said an amazing thing: "I have never witnessed war or brutality or anything like what you've described. And hopefully I never will. But we need to be reminded of both the worst and the best of what is human, for only then can we hope to heal it and change our world."

That day, the story had struck a universal chord that I will never forget, for as the older woman reminded us, we can, by telling our individual truths in the most authentic way, touch the universal truths that can change us all.

Thankfully, few of us have had to experience horrors like those of my student. I tell that story only to teach an important lesson about writing that this courageous storyteller conveyed to my class that day. Her lesson wasn't about violent encounters but about how, when we tell our stories with great authenticity, daring to craft our words so that our readers can enter into the private world of our experience, the result is intimate and transcendent.

In the years since that woman's story of mayhem, I have seen the same transformation occur many times over in classes I've taught. It is not *what* we tell in our stories that produces this amazing experience of transcendence so much as it is in the *how*. If we are willing to be fully authentic, inviting our readers into our inner world, we will strike that universal chord and change people's lives.

How do we do this? That's what this book is about. The author has generously shared her craft with us—what we must do to get started and how to keep going. In between there is excellent coaching in the craft, telling us how beginner as well as more advanced writers can make their stories move readers so that they come back again and again to our writings. But one of Lisa's most compelling messages has to do with finding our own voices and embracing what we are about. Lisa's wisdom as a memoirist and teacher of memoir writing comes through on every page. She supports us in the process of writing what we have lived, savoring the "second tasting" of our lives, the delayed reactions that are the source of our own "shimmering images."

—Hal Zina Bennett, author of *Write From the Heart: Unleashing the Power of Your Creativity*

By being the curator of our images, we care for our souls.

—Thomas Moore

INTRODUCTION

You've always wanted to write a story about your life. You've been planning to do it, telling family and friends you are going to do it . . . but you haven't done it.

Why not?

The answer is usually an apology of some sort, a sad tale of enduring hope and the busyness of your life.

What I've discovered, traveling around the country, teaching thousands of people to write stories about their lives, is that it isn't lack of desire or even busyness that keeps people from getting their stories down on paper. It's a sheer lack of know-how.

And frankly, the books currently available for aspiring memoirists fail to spell out a simple process: one-two-three.

Shimmering Images: A Handy Little Guide to Writing Memoir does that. It gives you the steps without a lot of fancy mumbo jumbo about literature and books you haven't read and never will.

I don't focus on other memoirs because they are not the point when you are learning how to do this. You need to stay focused on your own life so you can snatch up forgotten memories, avoid the intimidation that comes from reading more practiced writers, and sidestep the natural tendency to get swept away into the lives of other writers.

The point is *your* life.

Shimmering Images spells out a technique to get straight to the heart of your life, where the richest material resides. Then it shows you how to structure a memoir.

Plain and simple.

There are three parts to this book.

Part 1 talks about ideas behind writing a memoir, like why you need to pen your story and why you have the right to speak your truth.

Part 2 introduces Shimmering Images—the magic key to everything—then charts a simple step-by-step process for narrowing your focus, capturing your most powerful stories, and using them to construct the framework of a memoir.

Part 3 gives you a quick look at some of the craft of writing—tools, I call them—but only the stuff that will help you hone your memoir, not a lot of other stuff, useful to a writer, surely, but not necessarily pertinent to this process.

It's that simple, my friends.

And then the book is done. I'm out of here, and you keep using the process for the rest of your life. It's my gift to you—short, sweet, and, yep, simple: Lisa's three s's.

Why am I passionate about giving you this process?

That's pretty simple, too.

I believe writing memoir is the most effective way to change the world. Sounds lofty, I know, but honestly, the way I see it, when you write your story, you codify a truth about past experience.

That act changes you, opens up new, stunning possibilities for your future, and when witnessed by a reader—if you've done your job well and written with authenticity—the sheer act of sharing your truth allows that reader to claim her own truth. She codifies her story; someone witnesses that. And on and on we go.

If we write bighearted, compassionate stories, we have the chance to model forgiveness, to get beyond the old tales of past events; we have the chance to change the way people perceive their experiences. I can't think of a better way to spend my energy on Planet Earth, and since I know this process works, I simply love handing out these exquisitely refined tools.

It took a lot of years to get these tools down to the basics, I'll tell you that. Fact is, I've been perfecting this for as long as I've been a writer—through teaching full-time at universities, leading workshops from New York to Los Angeles, coaching clients across the country who are writing books, and instructing season after season of classes for the Extension Writers' Program at UCLA. A friend asked me to estimate how many students I'd worked with over the years, sharing the idea of Shimmering Images and helping them write their stories. "That's a tough one," I said, but I put some thought into it and decided five to six thousand people would be a conservative estimate. I know the bulk of those students got what they needed from this technique to craft a story about their life, a story that made a difference, and this brings me joy.

How did I get started with this memoir technique?

I began just like you: with talent, burning desire, and an unrelenting drive to pursue my dream of writing and publishing. About ten years ago, after fifteen-plus years of apprenticeship, my memoir *Hawk Flies Above: Journey to the Heart of the Sandhills* was published by Picador USA. It got some great reviews and won comparisons to the work of Annie Dillard. But even before that I'd started teaching what I was passionate about—how to speak your truth and turn it into a story. For more than twenty-five years I've been laser focused on the creative process and the craft of writing personal stories because that exploration spoke to my soul, called me, over and over again.

What I've gleaned from all this work is such a tight format for capturing and writing your stories that I don't need much more than one hundred pages to explain it.

And you don't need more than that to learn it.

Here it is. *Shimmering Images: A Handy Little Guide to Writing Memoir*. It's lyrical, playful, direct, and to the point, a pristine snapshot of the process writers use to illuminate the truth of their lives and write a story people will dash out to buy.

Bottom line: I could wax philosophic and analytic for pages, dragging out this book, but I don't want to waste your time. All I want to do is show you how to put your story together, and to get you writing.

The inspiration stage is fragile and elusive, and courting it is an art, so let's not waste it. Let's get to the juice.

Life is short.

Your stories are waiting, and I'm excited about helping you reach your dream.

PART I

The Ideas Behind
the Process

MEMOIR VERSUS AUTOBIOGRAPHY

Writing stories about your life is like plying the waters of some familiar yet exotic sea. It is the act of casting your sails for adventure.

Imagine it: The sun melts in a thousand shades of orange on a long horizon as your tiny craft cuts through swells, undaunted by the gathering challenge, because out in the haze awaits—you can see it—the dream of your story, the possibility of immortalizing your life experience, of speaking the truth of what you have seen, and heard, and felt.

This can be a long voyage, full of tempest, but I know of no other that can net such riches, for when you write a memoir you change your life. When you set down a truth about the past, a new future dawns.

Yet, before you begin this process, you need to understand what a memoir really is. We can't set sail on this adventure unless we're in the same boat, so let's get clear: Life stories fall into two big clumps. There's memoir and there's autobiography.

What's the difference?

Memoir involves the whittling away of a whole lot of stuff that you have lived and a focusing on one slim section, full of power, that demands to be told. This section may be told chronologically, but it does not necessarily have to be, if the story itself would best be served by some different approach. (You'll learn about structure in part 2 of this book.)

Autobiography is an overview of your entire life told chronologically from the "I was born" stage to the "and here I am now" stage.

For the purposes of this book, I am dealing with the slice-of-life memoir in which you identify one potent period and you explore it through vivid imagery, honest voice, stunning compassion, and a deep awareness of the larger issues at play that guide your story in a subliminal way—myth, metaphor, and current issues of the day. In this book we are not working with the autobiography.

In the process I will lead you through in this book, I encourage you to work with childhood stories, because they are ripe with material. Certainly you can apply this same process to any other segment of your life. It's simply an approach you are learning. It can be used again and again.

That said, I do believe the most successful memoir is written about periods of our life that are further away in the mists of memory.

Why?

Because you have some distance from the time period you are exploring. You need that depth of perspective to make sense of the events. Distance gives you wisdom, alternative views, and the possibility of compassion, all elements central to emotionally moving and exciting stories about your life.

Setting sail on this voyage of writing stories about your life, or stories that I call memoir, puts you squarely in the territory of what people in the publishing industry call narrative nonfiction. And it's good to know a little bit about that body of water.

Why do they call it narrative nonfiction?

Because in this form of writing you narrate (tell a story) about something that actually happened (nonfiction).

Narrative nonfiction has a gazillion other shapes besides memoir and autobiography, and you might hear about them in a conversation or read about them in an article. Here are some of them, with brief definitions:

- **Literary nonfiction:** A name given to writing that narrates a story using many of the devices of literature to make the writing poetic
- **Creative nonfiction:** A term referring to the use of creative writing techniques mixed in with a nonfiction story, often making the result seem like a novel
- **Essay:** A name given to a piece of personal writing in which the voice of the writer is prominent and which makes some kind of big, or subtle, point
- **Literary journalism:** A term used if the written story includes a kind of journalistic reporting about the world

Whatever the mix of writing techniques used, we have to agree on a term we will use here, together, on this journey, and because I teach a variety of techniques for writing your story— techniques that incorporate literary devices, creative writing skills, the logic of the essay writer, and the reporting of the journalist—and because I insist on teaching a slice-of-life story format, I use the term "memoir."

Memoir comes in many sizes and shapes. What I urge you toward in *Shimmering Images* is a kind of writing that

- Drives the reader forward to find out what happens
- Sings with the honesty of your individual voice
- Reads like a novel in places
- Offers reflective wisdom, in your authentic voice, that touches hearts and taps into the larger world out there, offering opportunities of interest for many readers

Don't worry, I'll teach you how to do these things. One step at a time.

2

CLAIMING YOUR VOICE

To write compelling memoir, you must first believe you have the right to speak, the right to tell your story, to be heard. You have to believe the story you are telling is important, key to your understanding of life and key to others'. For some, this is the highest wall to climb in writing stories about your lives, because too often you have been told that what you think, feel, and have experienced doesn't matter. You may spend a good part of the first few chapters of *Shimmering Images* battling—both inside yourself and in discussions with family and friends. It may come up again and again, stopping you as you progress. That's okay. I expect it. You should expect it, too.

I can imagine you right now, holding this book and thinking: Who am I to tell my story? Who cares? Who will listen?

Right?

Yep, that's part of the process. We deal with it and move on.

In my classes and workshops this is always the first order of business. Expect insidious doubt to rear its head as you scratch away the layers of convention that keep you from telling the truth of your life. Expect it to keep coming back. Greet it. And then get on with the next chapter. That's what you must do, because of course your life does matter, and the stories you write about your life are some of the most important work you can do in the world, because once you have written those stories, you will have changed your life.

So, expect that nasty little naysayer to show up. Refuse to let it silence the storyteller in you. Push forward. Keep reading these chapters. You will get a story written by the end of this book.

First you must claim your life. You must believe in every fiber of your being that you have the right to your reality: the way you interpret how things happened, the way you remember them. It doesn't matter in the world of this book, in the world of art and creativity, in the world we are creating right here, how other members of your family remember the year you were twelve, or how an old lover says that day on the lake unfolded, or how friends report that last evening at the dinner table.

In another place and time, those interpretations might be of importance (and maybe you will even work some of those conflicting views into your final written story). But right here and right now, what is central is that you know your truth—the version that resonates in your bones, electrifies the very skin of your being—is the one truth that will make your writing soar, that will grab readers by the throat and keep them coming back again and again to hear your voice tell them how it was.

3

TRUTH VERSUS FACT

Let's talk about truth. This subject will pop up again and again as you work on your stories. It's a valid discussion for the writing of life stories. Just remember: Every time it appears and you begin to question yourself and what you are writing, come back and read this chapter.

So okay . . . there you are working along, writing your stories, and you hear yourself saying, "But if my sister doesn't remember it the way I do, then what's the truth?" Or your lament may go like this: "If I make up conversation, it can't be factual, right? I kind of remember what happened that day, but do I have the words right? Am I writing memoir?" At this point you spiral into confusion, self-doubt, and get lost in worry and dread. I've watched this happen over and over with writers.

Let me say simply: There is the small truth of fact, and there is the larger truth you create when you make art.

Storytelling is art.

Making a story from life experience reflects a serious investigation of the human condition. When you use all the skills of the storyteller to write a story that seeks universal connections, that links your life to the lives of other humans, you take your experience beyond the act of simply reporting facts.

When you make a truth with story, you use the timeless skills of the storyteller to give the reader an experience that will change his life. That is why we write stories, to take ourselves and the reader into a new realm where the spirit can be repaired. That's what story does: It addresses the soul in some elemental way far beyond the lining up of minuscule details.

Story, the essence of narrative, is art. Writing life stories borders on the mystical because you, the writer, become the master of reality. You make sense of chaos. You bring order to life events through narrative; you attach meaning to events. That act is more than reporting facts; it is an act of creation. Art is creation. Memoir is art.

Get this clear: Writers of life stories are not journalists. The key reason for your work is not to report facts. Your responsibility does not lie in getting the facts right at the expense of truth— some deeper reality accessed and presented through the craft tools of the discipline of writing, tools that give you the power to create universal connections.

Facts over emotional truth is not the point.

Writers of memoir are storytellers, and the point of a personal story is to make a truth that resonates for you, that closes the experience around a narrative and brings it to completion. Narrative (story) that has a beginning, a middle, and an inevitable close (an end) is a kind of art that soothes the soul. That is what we are doing here. That is what I am teaching you to do.

Certainly you do whatever you can to get the facts as correct as possible: What was the name of the town? How many years did Peter live across the street? Was it a Buick Electra? What did your grandmother say that day? You do the research necessary to fill in the factual gaps: You talk with participants, weighing their feedback with your own; you look it up online or in a book; you plumb your memory.

After all the confirmation of facts, remember that in the end it is your truth created from your memory and your experience.

Your memory serves up the past in the way it does for a complex set of reasons that have to do with who you are and what you value. So, yes, you do everything humanly possible to get the facts right, according to you, and then get on with it, remembering that what you are really doing here by writing your life stories is recording the deep resonant, honest, compassionate truth that resides inside your heart, that links your experience to the experiences of hundreds of other humans on this planet. And you have the right to do that. You have the right to be heard.

4

HONESTY

What do I mean by honesty in a book about writing life stories, after I've told you memory is faulty and you have the right to what you remember, after I've told you your truth is bigger than facts? What could I possibly mean?

Honesty in the writing of life stories means telling the truth of your life experiences and not dressing those stories in silence, vagueness, or lies geared to protect other people.

Honesty of this sort does not give you license to be brutal and hateful toward other people; it simply means that having claimed your right to speak, you must tell the truth of what you have experienced.

Your job as a memoirist is not to protect other people at the expense of your own truth.

Neither is it to blame, point fingers, or savage other people.

Your job as a memoirist is to claim your own truth, to accept responsibility for your actions, and to make sense of the actions of others in the context of a story.

Many people I work with in my classes and workshops are more concerned with protecting others than writing about their lives, and yet they sit before me frustrated and yearning, wanting nothing more than to be honest, to be heard. Still, they stop themselves, for the sake of everyone else in their lives—living or dead. They honor others more than they honor themselves.

How many times have I heard: "But what will my aunt Millie think?" (Fill in the name of your choice.) "Will I be sued?" "I don't want to hurt anyone."

The fact is Aunt Millie will think whatever she wants to think regardless of what you do.

And the chances of getting sued are the least of your concerns, because first you need a manuscript. Worrying about such matters at this stage of the process is simply a way to stop yourself from writing.

I've always been able to tell the writers who will finish a memoir from those who won't. The people asking the questions about Aunt Millie and legal ramifications are erecting a roadblock right in front of their feet. They have tricked themselves into believing everyone else is more important than they are. That's easier to do than stepping up to the hard work of inspecting your life and crafting it into a book. Sometimes it's easier to be mute; any reason to stay mired in the fear of speaking and the imagined consequences of speaking can look like an island to a man adrift at sea.

And about that issue of hurting people. If you write with balance, honesty, and compassion you won't hurt anybody. You might open some people's eyes to the effects of their actions, but what's wrong with that? The act of making memoir, of crafting narrative from life experience, is about transforming your life and giving others the tools to do the same. The way I look at it, why not be an agent of change? But do it with grace. Memoir written with a vulnerable understanding of the complexities of what it means to be on this human path rarely hurts those characters who people its pages; instead, such memoir enlightens.

For all readers still honoring others above themselves, here are five fundamentals about honesty in the writing of life stories:

1. You have the right to speak. If you are still doubting it, that's okay. I said you would. But remember Lisa's bedrock principle of writing memoir: Being human accords you the right to be heard. Come back and read this chapter every time you doubt it.

2. If you have the confused notion you are honoring others by remaining silent, consider this: The only way you honor anyone or anything outside yourself is by first honoring yourself. Then you can walk with integrity in the world. Once you have personal integrity, you have the power to honor all outside yourself.

3. You must voice your stories to get beyond them. That's why we create stories from events and tell them to people—to make sense of what happened. Stories order the chaos of our lives. But if you do not write those stories, they may remain confused inside your body—a splatter of potent events on the map of your life, bugging the daylights out of you, year after year. If you don't line them up in some pattern (narrative) that offers grace for all involved and then eject that narrative from your body through the physical act of writing it down, you will never be able to get on to other things in your life. You will remain stuck in the old story, grinding down into it with repetition. You won't be open to all the new, fantastic stuff waiting for you beyond the edge of that clunky old version of the truth until you've packaged up the old stuff and made from it a narrative that completes it for your psyche.

4. If the other people in your life want to write their stories, make their own narratives, they are welcome to do that. Give them a copy of this book. Smile at them.
5. And remember, their truth is as valid as yours . . . it's just not yours. It's theirs. Smile again at them.

Being honest means really looking at your stories and making sure they are big. Being honest has to do with compassion, for yourself and others. And compassion is big—it's one of those emotions that take true humanity to exhibit. It requires that we get outside the small, judgmental mean-spiritedness that we may carry in our bones, every single day.

We can't be truly honest if we aren't being compassionate.

Compassion is so important in this process it occupies two separate chapters in this book: "Compassion 101" and "Compassion 102," coming up right now.

5

COMPASSION 101:

BECOMING GENEROUS

Getting to the kind of truth and honesty that will define your story as different from all others—making it a story people will grab and read—is more complicated than simply declaring your version correct and writing it.

Getting honest with yourself about things that have happened in your life means ripping away the illusion of what you've always told yourself.

Getting honest means learning compassion for the people in your life whom you would rather demonize.

Getting honest means coming to terms with your shared humanness, seeing all the players with empathy, and that includes yourself.

This kind of clear-eyed, balanced vision is one of the skills that will allow you to write a story that goes beyond stereotypes and small definitions of circumstances—same-old blaming, self-deprecating tales of misfortune.

This authentic approach will help you crack open your experience and find in it the universal stuff that links your life to all other people. And that, of course, is what people want to read:

"How is this writer's story like mine?" the reader asks. "How can I learn about my life from hers?"

Sometimes readers don't even know that is what they are asking when they pick up a book about another person's life. It's subliminal. But it is one of the main reasons readers come to memoir: to find out how they can live a better life by witnessing the mistakes and victories, the wisdom garnered, and the humility displayed by one of their fellow humans.

What they don't want is a repetition of their own self-flagellation and finger-pointing crap. They want a hero who uplifts them and shows them the way.

Sound simplistic? In some ways it is. We humans want to be shown examples of how to live a better life.

Here they are, the basics of compassion that will make your stories more believable to readers:

View events through the eyes of other characters.

Mix those versions in with your own; for example, you might write:

I always believed my sister was selfish. She never shared things and sometimes she locked her bedroom door. She wouldn't even share herself. Years later she told me, "Mom used to go through my things." Sis knew Mom was looking for "ammunition," she called it. It's true, they did fight a lot, but I don't know. Mom didn't go through my things, or at least I don't think she did.

What happens in this example is rather than blaming a character in the story for behaving in a way that felt hurtful, the writer allows the possibility of a more complicated truth. This makes the story more interesting and more readable, because it's not black-and-white: me good, her bad.

Be gentle with yourself in your story; no one wants to identify with a narrator who beats himself up (and that's what readers do; they identify with the narrator of a story; it's part of the reading experience).

When you can be generous with your characters, the people in your stories become more than stock characters used to shore up anger or fear.

When you can be generous, your claims about what happened become more believable. It's called balance. If you only point and blame, no one will believe you, but if you offer the possibility of an alternate interpretation, the reader is more likely to see it your way.

6

COMPASSION 102:

TRANSFORMING EXPERIENCE

Plain and simple, here's what I'm asking you to do:

1. Claim your version of what you think happened; plant a flag and brazenly announce your truth to the world.
2. Consider the possibility that your story of past events could be made more delicious, in the written world of story, with some balance, with a bigger view of the landscape that is your life.

Sound contradictory? Maybe. But it's not, really. In the world of written stories, it's the way to win readers.

This doesn't mean I've changed my stance on your right to speak or be heard. It means as a teacher of memoir I know what works and what doesn't. I know that in the world of written stories the truths we present to readers ring most believable when they are fashioned to include new insights we couldn't see when events transpired.

Remember, you don't have to run out and buy lunch for the characters in your stories or build a memorial to them. You don't have to declare them your best friends. You simply need to consider the possibility that they are human, too, and maybe they were coping with their own set of experiences as best they could when their life careened through yours.

If we writers are able to do this, we can begin to see new interpretations for our stories. And if we can see, even glimpse for one flashing moment, those new interpretations, we have the opportunity to write a bigger story than the tight, small one we have been carrying around repeating in our heads and to other people. Or both.

What you will discover, if you take this path in your writing, is that when you get to the place inside yourself where you are able to claim your right to speak and where you are willing to be bone honest with yourself, to re-envision what the trail of events might mean, you will be able to write the kind of story that makes people weep, and laugh, and keep turning the pages. Because what you will be writing is a story that transforms experience on the page, and when that happens and people read it, they transform, too, and that is addictive.

We want to be moved by art.

We want to be changed.

How do you get there as a writer of memoir?

1. Write a first draft of the story. Pour it all out, the rip-roaring joy, the ecstasy, the confusion, the anger, the sadness.
2. Put the story away; sit on it for a few days, weeks.
3. Pull it out and reread the story.
4. Ask yourself if your tale is fair to all the players.

5. Ask another writer, or trusted friend, to read your story and tell you if the story feels true, and generous, and non-blaming.

6. If necessary, scratch around inside your soul, look for a larger truth, get bigger than yourself, invite compassion, even if you have to write: "It grates my soul to say this, but I know now Mom was showing me a way to be in the world in the only way she knew." With these words you are at least acknowledging the possibility that the mother character in the story was human, too, and trying in her own muddled way to help a daughter. At least it's a bigger approach than simply writing paragraph after paragraph that says in essence: "That damn jerk ruined my life." Blame. Blame. Blame. Nobody wants to read it. I repeat: Nobody wants to read it.

7. Once you've come to terms with the possibility of some alternative version of your long-held truth, played around with it in small pieces of writing—for your writing group, in a journal . . . whatever—write a second draft by revising your first draft, sandwiching in fresh insights as you go.

8. Ask a writing buddy if the new version of the story has gotten bigger in spirit. If she is a good buddy she will tell you; she will guide you to the next right place of compassion, showing you where her heart was glad and where she wanted to stop reading because it was still too self-pitying or angry.

Here's the truth about memoir: Real stories are complicated, and they are complicated because the players in the story have complicated desires, dreams, and passions, which, exactly like life, weave into a tapestry of contrary, conflicting goals—like people we know and move with through the everyday world.

That's what makes life rich and frustrating and joyous and tragic. Those people out there aren't simple. And so a story about your life cannot be a simple: I did this, he did that; I'm the good guy, he's the bad guy. The best memoir is like the most elegant novel—a reflection of real life, laced with complexities of character and told by a compelling narrator. We just use the craft of writing a tad bit differently than our cousins the novelists.

PART II

The Process

7

SHIMMERING IMAGES

Let's start at the beginning: First you must get the stories out, and you will do that in little pieces.

I do not expect you to sit down and reel out five, ten, or sixty thousand words of tidy prose. I don't even expect you to reel out one page of tidy prose. You may do that—hoorah for you!—but most people don't. I don't, and none of my writer friends do, either. We fumble around trying to figure out what it is we are hankering to say and how best to say it, spewing messy draft after messy draft. That is the process of writing life stories. That's how we find the way to the true heart of meaning.

The way I teach memoir writing is to lead you along at a slow pace so that the story can go deep and in the process you can focus on the exquisite dance between what you are doing as an artist choreographing a large and potentially transformative work of art and as a craftsperson working the tools of the craft of writing.

To begin that slow dance, to find the small pieces, I must introduce you to Shimmering Images. A Shimmering Image is one of those memory pictures you've had for years. This is the most basic unit I use in teaching memoir. This is bedrock. You must have this before you can take another step forward.

Where did Shimmering Images come from? I made them up a long time ago—not the images, of course. I simply named something I saw in my head, something I used in my writing process, something that worked for me, and it worked so well for everyone I shared it with that I've continued using it. I've shared it with thousands of writers coast to coast for twenty years, in workshops and online courses, at writing conferences and art centers, and in college classrooms.

A Shimmering Image is a memory that rises in your consciousness like a photograph pulsing with meaning—standing in the side yard of your house talking with your neighbor, the sun angling in from the east, you notice her age, you notice the gray in her hair, you hear the sprinklers in the background, the sun is hot on your forehead. And that's all there is to it. Or you see an image of your dad slapping his best friend on the back, his head rearing back; you hear his barking laugh puncture the air. Your dad's teeth are so straight. And that's all the Shimmering Image consists of. Or there's that moment you remember riding your bike, looking over at the Mills house, slamming into the mailbox, and the next thing you know you are on the ground in a jumble of gravel and hair and scraped knees. Each one of these moments resides whole in your mind. You've remembered it a million times. It seems to have nothing that comes before it, nothing that follows. It exists alone, like a sepia-toned photo on a white wall. You have thousands of these images inside yourself. You remember them when you are walking the dog, practicing your golf swing, swimming, washing dishes, taking a shower, or sitting on the porch watching evening roll down your street.

These Shimmering Images are the source of your most potent stories. I am convinced of this. That's why I say they shimmer. They have energy; if you squint at them you will see the edges of the image shimmer, wiggle with potential, like one of those heat waves rising from a long hot highway across desert in the center of summer.

This shimmering is the energy of the story that waits inside the image to be told. That's why you have remembered these images all these years. Over and over they come back, knocking at the door of your creative soul, waiting to shed light on your life, waiting to share the wisdom that resides inside them.

At this point you should know what I'm talking about. You should have a whole bunch of these Shimmering Images floating around in your head.

Good.

Hold on to them.

Make a few notes so you'll remember them—in an electronic file or handwritten in your journal, someplace where you keep story ideas. These images flitting into consciousness are stories waiting to happen. You may not capture them with words right away as you work through this book, but you will have them as material for other projects, which you can write after you've learned this process.

Remember that whatever you write the first time through this book is just one story. You can apply this same process over and over again and come up with tons of written stories. So, hang on to all those Shimmering Images. Whenever one shimmies into the front lobe of your consciousness, jot it down in your ever-growing file of "Stories That Need to Be Told"—even if all you have time for is one or two words. Capture it: pears, swimming pool, four-leaf clovers, fresh-mown grass, refrigerator boxes.

Don't let the image slip away.

That Shimmering Image has come back to you for a good reason, and you have to trust that it knows the reason, even if you don't.

The following two chapters—"The Mountaintop" and "Memory Maps"—show you ways to find various jumping-off places (beginnings) for a slice-of-life memoir and for finding the Shimmering Images that will become the building blocks of that story.

Have fun exploring the terrain of your life.

8

THE MOUNTAINTOP

The Mountaintop is an exercise that will help you with the structure of your stories. It's a way to find a beginning from the imaginary view of a mountaintop. I've used this exercise for a long time. Again, I simply named something I saw in my mind's eye, something I found I was doing in my own process as a writer. And like the Shimmering Image, it worked for people I shared it with. So, here it is for you:

Every story about your life, every slice-of-life memoir, needs to begin somewhere. To be a story that people will want to read it has to serve up to the reader the possibility of a "problem" that will be "solved" during the course of the story.

Now, I don't mean necessarily a blatant problem, like the dead body that turns up in the first paragraph of many mysteries, but rather the possibility of the reader following a narrator as he unravels the impact and comes to terms with some life complexity. In other words, a rousing tale of you getting to be the hero of your own life.

Bottom line: Stories are about challenges—*trouble,* as I like to call it—and the working through of those challenges. This is the process readers love to witness.

"How will she [you, the protagonist, the narrator of your tale] figure this one out?" the reader asks himself. "What will she do?"

Incredulous, or heartbroken and wondering, wondering, wondering, he reads on to find out what happens.

This is the process we watch in American movies: There is a key character who has a problem and we, the eager viewers, popcorn munch our way through a couple hours of watching that person come to terms with the problem. It's what novels do, too, sometimes in a circuitous and messy, wildly diverted, distracting, and engaging way. But sooner or later the novel brings us to the end of the character's journey and to whatever that character has figured out about her life by taking that journey.

Memoir needs to do the same thing: We, the readers, go on a journey with a character who explores a segment of his life. We watch as he makes that journey and comes out the end of it with something to show for having made the trip.

How do you get started doing this? First, you must get clear that the tale you are going to tell is a slice of life, rather than an autobiography. Second, you locate the source of some "trouble" in your life. That trouble becomes the jumping-off place for exploring a slice of life. Your Shimmering Images associated with the "trouble" will reveal the meat of your story. In the ensuing chapters, you will learn how to piece this whole thing together so it makes sense and touches readers' hearts.

The purpose of the Mountaintop exercise is to help you find a bunch of places in your life where you encountered "trouble," where you came up against one of life's challenges. This listing is not about solving those challenges. The Mountaintop is about gathering them.

You can think of this exercise as a way to gather story begin-nings, embryonic stuff from which books can be created: the hurdles you have surmounted, difficulties you have overcome, challenges you've stepped up to, victories you've relished (because even victory signals change, and change signals a potential story). These events are the seeds of epic memoir.

To begin . . . I want you to imagine that you are on the top of a mountain looking down into a river valley below. Use some place you've hiked to, once upon a time, or meandered past—an overlook or pastoral landscape—or if you live in a city and loathe the out-of-doors, conjure up some movie image, a long shot of mountains and a river arcing and bending in the valley below.

Get yourself to the top of one of those peaks.

Imagine the river reflecting the silvery blue of the sky, the sting of the sun, the beckoning shade of the pines nearby, the scent of those pines wafting on hot air. . . .

Now think of the events in your life after which everything was different, events after which your life flowed in a direction different from the life you lived before the event. Some of these moments you can only perceive from a distance; sometimes we don't realize our life has changed because of an event. Sometimes it's so subtle that only years later are we able to look back and say, "Ahhh . . . that's where it started." That's why memoir often takes years to manifest.

Your Mountaintop events could be as simple as the first time your best friend told you she was having sex. You were still a vir-gin and did not understand the siren call she felt to that boy, night after night. Your relationship with the little girl down the street changed; you moved forward into a future walking a path that separated you from your best friend. How was it different? Why?

Or how 'bout the first time you had sex?

The day you gave up your bike and took up driving a car?

High school graduation?

Each of these events may seem small in the whole scope of your life, but they are ripe for exploration.

A Mountaintop event can be a big event, too: the death of a parent, moving to a new city, marriage, divorce, the birth of a child, any event that changed the direction of the flow of your life. Imagine that river below you in the valley with lots of bends and eddies. Each curve in the body of that river is a turning point in your life, an event after which you lived differently, after which your life flowed, either abruptly or almost imperceptibly at first, in an unfamiliar direction.

Simply make a list of these events. Aim for twelve. Certainly you can come back to this exercise over and over again and add moments to the list. But for now, record twelve.

These are not intended to be written stories. List them like groceries you would buy at the store: one word or a short phrase. Your list might have events like these:

- Moved to Boulder that summer with Martin
- Grandma and Grandpa bought place in Miami
- Mom and Dad divorced
- Made the basketball team
- Followed Dad to the mill after high school
- Started piano lessons
- Got first car
- Won art scholarship
- Met Dave
- Married Kate
- Rented the house on A Street

- Jack born
- Sold the family farm
- Pammy got sick
- The boat accident
- Dad died
- Divorced Kate
- Traveled to Italy
- Saw first Broadway play
- Visited L.A.
- Got sober
- Lost job
- Learned to ski
- Joined team at the hardware store
- Graduated from college
- Sold first magazine article
- Landed contract to build motels
- Kissed Bobby
- Closed deal with Harper Co.
- Took internship in Australia

Your list of Mountaintop events will be as individual as you are. Let it flow. Follow that river in your mind and observe the life-changing events that want to crowd along it. Don't judge them; watch them turn up and take note. You can sort them out later.

After you've let the events present themselves, you need a visual way to catalog them. I recommend a long sheet of paper. Butchers still have rolls, and you can purchase any length. Or tape together a bunch of sheets. If that's too much for you, draw the darn thing on the back of an envelope lying on the kitchen counter.

Draw that river as you see it snaking through the valley, and place along it, at each bend, an event that changed your life. Use colored pens to record your events, put a star or X at the curve in the riverbank, and write a word or short phrase to name the event. Draw a river long enough to accommodate all the Mountaintop events. It should look like a long snake with all sorts of scribbles adorning it.

Tack up your river on the wall above your writing space. Add to it when some new event surfaces in your memory.

Each of the events you place along that river represents a possible beginning for a story. Don't worry about how you are going to turn those events into stories that spark readers' hearts as they page into your tale. I'm going to walk you through that. Just know this: There is a simple way to mine these events for material. I will show you how to do that. To get to that stage, though, of mining the material and writing it, you have had to go through this process. Even if you don't "get" where we are going yet, you must check out the view from the Mountaintop; you must identify launch points, moments after which everything changed, places in your life where "trouble" was introduced to the story line.

For now draw that river, place along its banks the events you see down there in the valley, and move on to the next chapter. In "Memory Maps" you'll learn to locate Shimmering Images that will steer the way you shape your life-changing event into a piece of written memoir.

9

MEMORY MAPS

It's been so long since I first created the Memory Map exercise that I can't tell you how it came into being. What I do know is that over the years waves of students have rolled back to me and repeated similar words: The maps they drew in my classes changed their writing.

The Memory Map grows out of the Mountaintop. Together these two exercises lead you to a place where Shimmering Images surge into consciousness like a flood. When you reach this point, you are primed to collect your stories and let the material speak.

Because the Memory Map is critical to the process of accessing Shimmering Images, it is essential that you do it, that you understand how to do it, and that you be successful with it. It opens the door to a world that waits inside you where all your stories hang out. So, if there are any questions about this process, speak up. Really. Contact information is at the back of this book, or come to one of my workshops. I can't deliver your stories to you, but I can deliver you to your stories.

First, gather together the following supplies:

- The Mountaintop drawing you created in the last chapter with your key events stationed along the river. This is essential, so if you didn't make one, go back now and do it.
- At least two sheets of eight-and-a-half-inch-by-eleven-inch paper, but you may use something larger. Drawing paper is great, used in conjunction with your notebook. And even larger sheets for the map can be purchased at an art supply store, or there's that infamous butcher paper referred to earlier. Don't eat meat? Well, you can still check into some corner deli where they package meat or fish and buy a few feet.
- At a minimum, a pencil or pen, but I encourage you to use all sorts of writing tools. In the classroom, I show up with colored pencils, pens, and crayons. If you have them, use them. They can be great fun. And, yes, this *is* supposed to be fun. You are co-creating here—you and your inner child are making a doorway for all the information you have housed inside of you to come through into the practical world of writing.

Bottom line with this exercise: Use anything you can to enhance the visuals of your Memory Map. Color is always good, because like scent it enhances your ability to access memory.

The exercise consists of ten steps.

Step 1

When you have all the materials gathered, spend a couple minutes gazing at your Mountaintop picture. You are seeking one of the key events you placed there, along the banks of that river. Choose the one that jumps out at you. It either will be screaming: "Don't look at me. No. No. I'm invisible. Please leave me alone," or it will be flashing you a neon message that says: "Yeah, baby. Here I am. Me-me-me!"

Either will do, but I can give you a tip: The most audacious story waits behind the one trying to hide. That is the place where you'll find the most emotion, the most passion, and the most resistance. Resistance in the writing of personal stories is a catchword for *story-that-needs-to-be-told*. Whatever is behind the resistance has so much energy that you yourself, its author, are scared of it. Think what it would be like if you could harness its power. Hoover Dam on the Colorado River blown to smithereens.

Writing about your life is hard work. It requires you to be emotionally truthful, and truthful tales of the inner life are hard to get out, a little like digging embedded slivers from the soft part of your hand. It's no wonder you hide out from these stories, procrastinate, deflect. The tough stories aren't going anywhere, though, so when you are ready to write them, they will be waiting. And know this: When you decide to step up to those memories, address their patterns, and explore the myths they mirror, you will be on the verge of writing a big story.

For now, simply choose one of the events lining the banks of your river. Reach out with a pencil or pen to your Mountaintop exercise and put a star by that event; designate it officially and visually as the one you have selected, the one potent moment-after-which-everything-changed into which you are going to sink for the next few weeks as you mine it for material. All other events along the river can be set aside for now. But remember: They are all stories. Each one represents a place to which you can return later and begin this process again, crafting from that single event an entire world of story. Each is the source of dozens of Shimmering Images, which can fuel pages of writing. You could write for a long time and never fully mine all the material your Mountaintop exercise and the accompanying Memory Maps could generate.

Step 2

On another sheet of paper—notebook, journal, whatever works for you—write at the top of the page a catchphrase for the Mountaintop event you have chosen. It might be the phrase you wrote on the map itself:

- Grandma and Grandpa bought place in Miami
- Got first car
- Married Kate
- Sold the family farm
- Dad died

Below that phrase, and in writing, answer this question: Where were you living when this event took place? Be specific: the Craftsman bungalow in Bloomington, Illinois; a mountaintop cabin in the Sacramento Mountains of southern New Mexico; that apartment on the Upper East Side in Manhattan above the deli that always smelled of pastrami. The description needs to be as clear as possible. Saying simply "Tibet" is not enough. You need to say "the hut on the south slope of the hill ten kilometers from the village where I bought rice in that basket I now keep on the piano." Or "the house on Potter Street with the willow in the backyard and the bushes I hid under when I had that dog I called Fluffy but which my mother named Edward." Or "that cottage I lived in on Nantucket the year after my husband died of cancer, when I took a leave from my job and worked on the novel I'd always wanted to write." You understand. Conjure the place with specificity.

Step 3

With your one selected event and place in mind, turn to a large sheet of paper and draw a rough map of the house, cabin, hut, apartment. Locate trees and streets and parking lots, the buildings or landscape viewed from windows, the neighbor's house, shops, a sidewalk, patio, stream, bridge, the acres of maples and oaks— anything significant in your memory. (Alongside this overview map, you can even do a "zoom-in" map of the inside of the house, the bedroom, bath, your favorite chair in the living room, or a "zoom-out" map of the neighborhood, town, or region.) Play with this. Simply put down on paper in visual form those details that come to you and feel significant. Do this until you have thoroughly enlivened that place in your heart and mind, until it is vivid and as real as it was the last time you walked out the door or flew away from that city. Get it distinct in your mind, right down to the cupboard where the toothpaste was stored, your favorite mug, the design of the comforter that covered the bed, the color of morning light as it cascaded in the kitchen window.

And be cognizant: As you create your map, you will have sensations of stories come over you, memories. Shimmering Images will rise.

Step 4

As these Shimmering Images appear, be ready with another sheet of paper to jot them down. Or you can locate them right on the Memory Map. Note them in the places where you remember them, with one or two words that help you capture the memory, or list them on that other sheet of paper. You don't write a story at this point. Simply gather the Shimmering Images. The quick label you apply will be your path back to the Shimmering Image later. But be sure the words capture the moment. Why? These Shimmering Images can be like dreams; they can slip away in the light of day. Don't assume you will remember the Shimmering Image later.

Whatever system you develop with your Memory Map is fine; create something that works for you. The point is to conjure with the map the place where you lived when you went through the event taken from the Mountaintop exercise and in the process to let the Shimmering Images associated with it rise and wiggle into life before your eyes, filling you with that time and place, and with the memory of who you once were. Record, with a word or two, those images. They will be the prompts you come back to later as you write installments of your memoir and even later as you craft it into a story with forward movement.

Do not worry about what the images have to do with the original event. Do not concern yourself with their point, or why you are remembering them, or how you will use them. All such concerns are "editor mind" getting in your way, working overtime to shut you down with thinking about the process before you can even allow the process to happen.

Just draw and let the images rise. Take note of them.

What I am doing here is kicking you out of left brain, that master of the linear, and into right brain, the wizard of the holistic. Here is where your stories reside. Later you will need the skill of the left-brain organizer to shape those stories, but not now.

Step 5

When you have drawn the Memory Map and let at least a dozen stories bubble to the surface and you have captured them with a word or two, you can stop. Know that you can come back to this map at any time and locate new Shimmering Images. There will always be more you didn't discover the first time around, or the second, or third. Your Memory Map is a source of endless treasure. Do not throw it away. You will continue to work with it in the coming weeks. Tack it up on the wall next to the Mountaintop exercise and along with the accompanying list of Shimmering Images drawn from the map. Be sure to keep both the list and map within reach. Eye level is a good place. Then, each time you walk by you can gaze at it and conjure a new Shimmering Image, adding its notation to the Memory Map and its short identifying label to the list.

Let me be clear that you do not have to be an artist to create this map. I draw these Memory Maps in every class I teach, and I am not an artist. I use boxes and Xs, straight lines and circles, to indicate objects I put on the map. My perspective is regularly out of whack, and I don't care. Nor should you. None of that is important. It's not the point. Your goal here is not to create a museum-quality picture. What is important is that you allow yourself to become immersed in an interior world of memory about the place you are conjuring and to let the picture-stories rise.

Step 6

Now, with all that done, sit down at your writing table with plenty of paper, curl up in your favorite chair with your journal and a cup of tea, or head out with your laptop to the corner espresso bar and snuggle into the bay window among the discarded newspapers and magazines. With a cappuccino in hand and your list of identifying phrases nearby, begin.

Run your eye over the material on your list, as you did when you reviewed your Mountaintop exercise. Let the eye find one snippet, one Shimmering Image that jumps out at you. Like the turning points you located along the river in your Mountaintop exercise, some of these pivotal memories are going to shuffle into the corner of your mind, pull their trench coat around themselves, and feign distraction by burying their head in *The New York Times.* "Don't talk to me. I'm busy," they mutter. Others will wave their sun hat from the edge of the shore, beckoning you to walk with them in the water. Do as you like, but remember the caveat outlined earlier: Many of your best stories are the ones hiding in the corner, and the truly great piece of memoir must ultimately go into the dark and walk them out of that hidey-hole and into the light. In time you will explore each of these Shimmering Images, but for now, if your terrified friend wants to peruse *The New York Times* and hide in the comforting illusion of anonymity, let her. You'll be inviting her to remove the trench coat soon enough.

Step 7

With the first Shimmering Image you have selected, I want you to begin writing. Tell me the story. What happened? Where were you? Describe the setting, the characters, the smells and tastes. Don't worry about language or phraseology or spelling or anything, for that matter. Burrow into the image inside you and get it out on paper. Everything. Use the technique of freewriting advocated by many writing teachers today: Write swiftly and keep the hand moving. Don't stop. When you stop you immediately flip back into the left brain, the region of the Editor. When you keep your hand moving, you hang out with the Muse in the right brain. Believe me, this is a time during the creative process when you want to hang out with the Muse. Later your stalwart and ever-ready Editor will stand at attention. Her stunning skills will be put to good work. Be sure to remind her of this. Tell her you love her, give her a bite of biscotti, then invite her to nap.

There's no word limit on this part of the process, but try for at least three pages for each Shimmering Image. And more is better. At this point in the discovery process, go long. Brevity, honing, shaping, deleting can come later. It is easier to snip when you are shaping the story than to get yourself back to this white-hot moment of vision and to conjure again the initial passion. Include as many sensory details as possible. What that means is find the visuals in the picture and describe them with colors and shapes. Remember the smells and weave them in. Taste and smell will draw in a reader faster than anything else. You love to eat? So does your reader. Include food and you'll have your reader right on your shoulder salivating for more. And find those moments in the story when you felt the scratchiness of the wool sweater, the heat of your lover's chest, the dampness of a child's forehead. Describe how it felt. Describe what it evoked in your gut, in your solar plexus, in your heart.

Step 8

The only rule is don't stop writing, even for a second. Write: waiting, waiting, w-a-i-t-i-n-g until the next thought comes. The exact, fractional moment the hand stops moving or the fingers pause on the keys, the cranky editor in you flings open the door of your creative hut and yells, "What do you think you're doing?" And your fragile little creative self crawls under the desk.

Yep, it happens that fast.

When you have written everything about this image you can capture, choose another Shimmering Image from the Memory Map list and do the same with it. These Shimmering Images are meant to be first drafts, blazing remembrances written without self-consciouness or editing. Don't worry about getting it "right." And for heaven's sake, don't worry about punctuation. Write what comes to you. Quickly.

Don't stop until you have told everything you can remember, until it feels done, but be careful that you distinguish the difference between a Shimmering Image feeling done and the lethargy that creeps over you when you are approaching a difficult part of the remembrance, a part that frightens or shames. The feeling in your body will be different. Completion of a Shimmering Image feels like closure, a sinking down into an *ahhh* feeling, a recognition of a job well done. Distraction from that completion affects you differently. It's like a drug making you feel sleepy. Suddenly you need to close your eyes and rest. Or that distraction can come in the shape of a door slamming in your face, an Edvard Munch scream rising up your windpipe. Either one of these is not completion, and it must be written through. You must push the Shimmering Image forward through that stunning desire to stop and water the plants, make that phone call, check your e-mail.

You must push forward.

The ability to do this will distinguish whether you have what it takes to go the distance.

It's okay to be scared. It's human. It's okay to cry or feel pissed off. But you have to do that *as* you write. If you put the Shimmering Image aside and move on to an "easier" one, you will be teaching yourself that there is always an out. You have to step up to it. If you find this too overwhelming, I advocate forming a small group of friends who work through this process together. Gather in a coffee shop weekly, or in one of your living rooms. Give yourselves fifteen minutes to write each image, then move on to the next. Support from friends scribbling frantically to your left and right can be just the balm your frightened creative artist needs.

Step 9

Choose a third Shimmering Image, and do the same. Go boldly forward. Keep writing. Don't think about how these pieces fit together. Don't edit.

Did you hear me? No scratching out. No rereading. And don't think about how these pieces fit together. Not now.

I suggest writing these in threes. Each time you sit down to go at another Shimmering Image from your map, allow yourself enough time to work in threes. It was Pythagoras who said three was the perfect number—the golden triangle and all that; a three-legged stool is more solid than one with four legs. Trust me: Threes are good.

When you've written three, then you can go back and read them over, but it's not necessary, and this is definitely not the time to rewrite. Rather, going back is simply an opportunity to witness what you have written—no judgment—and a time to clarify any messy penmanship or lousy typing so later, when you come back to the material, you will know what it says and not stand there with your mouth hanging open, eyebrow cocked, wondering what "soidafonplnd" means.

After writing three Shimmering Images, get on to other things in your day.

As you are walking around doing those other things, the

material will simmer, become part of you in a new way, and blend with the larger process of creation that is cooking in your life.

Step 10

Tomorrow get up and write three more. And the next day, and the next . . . Only when you have generated many Shimmering Images will you be ready to approach the work of structuring your memoir.

If you know you can't control your need to fix and change, do not go back and read at this point in the process. To do so is a recipe for never getting beyond the first three stories of your book.

In chapter 12, you'll explore the basic ideas underpinning structure in a compelling slice-of-life memoir—architecture, I like to call it—or how all these Shimmering Images fit together.

In the meantime, let's take a look at how you can conjure more and more Shimmering Images and spin them through with lush details and the sensuousness of life. The following two chapters—"Personal Archives" and "The Larger World"—show you a couple ways to do this.

10

PERSONAL ARCHIVES

Memoir is about your life. It's about exploring the terrain of memory and seeing what truths that territory reveals. It's about recapturing images and finding meaning in them. To do these things means initiating a series of steps, the simplest of which is staring out the window and allowing memory to take up residence in the front of your brain, in that elegant salon where the images cavort and you relive them, with smiles and grimaces, no doubt, but the place where you first sift the stuff that makes up narrative nonfiction, the place where you start scouting for its gems.

That salon of the mind is the place from which you will ultimately dump those memories onto the page. It is also the place where you will charm a few of the reluctant memories out of the shadows and onto the dance floor for a spin with truth.

One way I get this whole process rolling is to crawl up onto a ladder, haul out the boxes, and rummage through my Personal Archives, all that stuff I save. I have always been a packrat. I have moved around the country so many times I have lost count, but always I have hauled my stuff with me. At various times in my life I have: (1) been appalled at that habit, (2) thought nothing of it, (3) thrown out boxes and cartons of stuff, pared down until I felt naked, and then (4) begun collecting again.

Of late, though, I have come to understand my stuff and my propensity for saving it in a different way: All that stuff amounts to a record of my life. The old journals, calendars, and daybooks, letters received and copies of letters sent (and now tons of electronic files of correspondence—letters and e-mails), chronicle how I lived my days, the choices I made, the feelings that rumbled through me, the places I went, the food I ate, and the friends with whom I laughed. I even have boxes of mementos—cocktail napkins, stones, pressed leaves, newspaper clippings, posters of events, movie tickets, concert programs. In one box I recently found a piece of paper with a pawprint on it of a dog that once occupied my heart.

What in heavens is all this stuff?

Like Shimmering Images, each of these things amounts to a doorway into a story. I see the cocktail napkin and I remember the sunny May day on the deck at that bar in Bass River on Cape Cod, and the boy I loved. I remember his wide hands, his chocolate eyes, his kind heart.

The leaves remind me of the fall I was in college and I took to pressing leaves and sending them to my aged grandmother with little notes of love. When I shuffle through this stuff, holding each item, perusing, remembering, a whole story rises up before my eyes, and I am alive inside its rich details. I can remember the girl I was in those days, the girl often lost to me now.

Calendars help me reclaim weeks, months, years gone missing. I locate where I lived then and exact occurrences come back to me, moments not as solid as a Shimmering Image that has swung back time and again, but moments lost to me until jogged in this way.

I use my Archives to stimulate the memories that have gotten stuck somewhere out of reach. All that stuff brings back the smells and sounds and tastes that often over time dull in our minds.

Not many years ago I was showering at our family cabin in the Sandhills of Nebraska and I reached up onto the shelf, seeing a bottle of hair rinse that looked familiar. I used to buy that brand. I hauled it down and pried open the spout. I gave the bottle a quick squeeze before inverting it, and the smell hit me like a baseball bat. There I was in the shower with my boyfriend when I was a student at Reed. There we were scrubbing our hair sharing the bottle of Flex. I hadn't remembered him that vividly in years, but the smell, like all that memorabilia I carry around in boxes, was a doorway into that time and place, to a man and his essence, to the girl I was in those days of sharing with him.

So I say to you: save, save, save. In this time of voluntary simplicity, if you are a writer of personal stories, resist the movement to pare down. Be a packrat. Join forces with other writer packrats, form a society heralding the benefits of packratting: Packrats International. This is exactly what you need to be doing. Get out your stuff and wallow in it; bring back your first year in college, the year your dad worked in Mississippi and commuted home on weekends. Haul out the photo albums and enhance this research with those iconic images. All of it together is your richest source for conjuring your personal material.

Imagine sitting at your desk, in your corner of the couch, at the kitchen table late at night. Let your hands explore that polished silver hat pin your great-grandmother wore to luncheons, plays, and concerts with your dashing and elusive great-grandfather. Slip your hand inside that worn baseball glove your father used in college. Imagine using the images that fill your mind to build a story.

Then move to the page and see what comes. If you feel you have run dry, dig more deeply into those boxes of stuff and see what stories shape-shift onto the screen of your mind.

11

THE LARGER WORLD

E very effective and moving piece of memoir is about more than your life and your interior experience of emotion. It is about the complexities of a place, the people who have paraded through your days, a social movement, politics, an issue like poverty, or aging, or the complex web of achievement and compromise that constitutes a career.

Weaving elements of this nature into a narrative about daily experience and emotion requires a great deal of finesse in terms of structure, story line, and voice, but if you step up to the challenge, the memoir you produce will be bigger than the small circle of your interior experience. And if your memoir is bigger than just your interior experience, if it includes the Larger World—references to issues that link us as humans—it will offer doorways for all sorts of readers who might not find meaning in your great-grandmother's hat pin or your dad's worn glove.

If you parallel your grandparents' story with a political movement, or focus on popular culture—the clothing people wore, the music they danced to, food that graced their tables, and the zeitgeist of the time—or if you weave into your personal story of growth and triumph a parallel story of growth and triumph experienced by a popular sports figure, then suddenly your story is bigger than just about you; it's about contemporary history, too. It's about the Larger World. More readers have the opportunity to locate a point of interest in your story when you expand its scope. They have a chance to find something that speaks to them in a way the story may not have spoken to them when it was focused solely on your intimate experience.

Certainly there are other ways to draw readers. The voice of the narrator alone can be so jazzy and full of personality that it captures readers' hearts, or the writer may make his writing so rich with the music of language, and textured with poetics, that we readers cannot help but be drawn into the sheer beauty of the craft, finding convergences in our journey with each step of the narrator's.

But some of us can't write like that. We aren't great stylists. Nor are we able to compose complicated and extended comparisons between the Larger World and our own world. Yet anyone can do some plain old research and learn about the time of which they write. Anyone can integrate references to sports and music, food, movies, or TV shows, radio programs, and events in the news, issues about race, gender, and money, war concerns, environmental concerns, problems right in her own hometown or neighborhood. Anybody, with a tad of effort, can find the Larger World connections surrounding his day-to-day experience and sprinkle them into the narrative.

All it takes is a little research. For many of you, looking through your Personal Archives will do the trick. It will bring back enough of the details you need to paint a place and the culture in which you lived, but maybe it won't be enough to remember the big baseball games of the era, or the favorite foods, or the names of the trees that grew in your town. In that case you need to go further. You need to be familiar with the library, or at least with the process of finding information on the Internet.

And even if little of this "research" finds its way into the final draft of your book, the sheer act of taking the time to consider the Larger World—the multitudinous details of a place and a time—can push you outside the vortex of me, me, me. It can help shift the tone of your story.

As memoirists, we have to remember that readers seek our stories in a quest to witness another human being coming to terms with the complexities of life. To identify with that struggle, readers have to have doorways into the story, and the way you provide those doorways is to link your story to aspects of human experience other people can identify with. This seduction of the reader can be done with stunning writerly voice or literary style, as mentioned, but even with that strength, the more you include elements of the world outside your personal howl, the more opportunity readers have to align their own experience with yours and find commonality in the content of your tale. Besides, it's not only the possibility of style readers are looking for in memoir; they are looking for a common thread of connection. All style and no content is like all cookies and no protein—fun for a while, but then you run out of steam and begin looking for something that nourishes on a deeper level.

The common thread we writers of memoir can offer readers is our life in the context of a larger experience that was shared by other humans. For example: the look and feel of a city during a particular era, its crime problems, the artists who directed its cultural life, musicians who populated its clubs, *along with* your experience moving through its streets, going to those clubs, tapping your foot to those iconic musicians, *and* living your individual life.

Or perhaps you grew up on a farm and you want to write about those years. Your personal story of family and crops and animals will be enhanced if you offer the bigger picture, too: some history of agriculture, notes on the weather during those years, background info on machinery and techniques, stories about water rights, anything that will allow the reader to see your personal journey in the context of a larger story.

I have clients writing about their individual journey through life but aligning those journeys with topics as diverse as a curmudgeonly horse, a life of catering adventures, and volunteer medical service during the 2004 tsunami in Indonesia. Yes, each story is at core about the narrator, but in each case the story is about so much more. Each story offers readers various doorways to enter the tale, join hands with the narrator, and walk together the experience the writer has lived. Along the way, not only do readers get to witness some new and engaging—funny, heartbreaking, eye-opening—stuff, but they also get to fire their own yearning with the struggles of the narrator searching for a bigger way to be in the world. That is the real gift of the Larger World for your memoir.

A practical strategy for making the Larger World part of your writing is to gather a lot of information about the time and place where you lived during the "slice of life" you are writing about.

- What major events were going on in the world at that time?
- How did people in your community respond to those events?
- What were the economic realities of the time?
- Why were they that way?

- How did people spend their free time?
- What styles and trends captured the popular imagination?
- What traditions were common?
- What music was popular?
- What did people read?
- What did they eat?
- What values did your community teach its children?

Considering questions like these helps you see your experience in a larger playing field and opens up possibilities for a more complex narrative.

You don't need to know what you will do with all the facts you gather, or which ones you will use in a final draft. You'll figure that out as you hone the structure. For now absorb a bunch of stuff about the world during the time you're writing about. Read old magazines, newspapers, biographies, histories. Watch DVDs, TV shows, movies. Listen to the music that was popular. Revisit the food through old cookbooks. Talk with strangers who lived during the same time. What were their experiences? What are their recollections? Make notes of anything that interests you. Read the notes several times, until the information is part of you. Put the notes away.

Then get specific and investigate the place you explored with your Memory Map. Talk to old neighbors. Rummage around in the local library's archives. Call relatives and ask them what they remember. Jot down the tidbits that catch your fancy. They will find their way into the story when you need them. If you don't have them, they never will find their way into your story, and your writing will be less rich and evocative.

I'm not going to fool myself into thinking that most people who want to write about their lives are going to spend weeks holed up doing intensive research like some scholar, jotting down notes in detailed format, but I am going to say that if you want to write a memoir that will appeal, it needs to be about more than your interior head space. Including the Larger World is one way to ensure that.

If you choose this avenue, go all out—master your place and time. Really learn it. Get it into your bones, by reading and viewing and asking questions of yourself and the material, by taking notes and reading those notes and lodging the information in the marrow of who you are, and by putting those notes aside, then, and getting on with your life.

When the tidbits of information you've gathered are pertinent to the tale you are unfolding, the writer in you will know when to dump the right fact here and there. If the information is part of who you are, it will simply pop out of you and onto the page, like the way a Shimmering Image tumbles out of you, like the way you remember the neighbor's Great Dane who stole your underwear off the clothesline. It's there when you need it.

Remember: You are not writing a research paper. Nor are you a journalist recording a balanced and objective story. But if you are smart about this part of the memoir process, you will see how making your story bigger than self will increase your odds of capturing an audience larger than the neighbor's dog and your children.

12

STRUCTURE

After you have written at least a dozen Shimmering Images, explored your Personal Archives, researched the Larger World, and written a few more Shimmering Images from that adventure, you will be ready to start thinking about structure. If you are writing a book, I recommend writing twenty to thirty Shimmering Images before moving on to the structure stage.

Why?

Because you need to let your muse do her magic. You need to let the imagination lead you to the core of your stuff *before* you let your logical mind dash into the room and try to *tell* you what this stuff is all about.

The fact is you don't know what this is all about in your logical mind. If you did, you would have figured it out years ago. Your myth-making mind, the mind that sees patterns in human experience, knows much more than the logical, fix-the-washing-machine brain. It knows things in a way you cannot herd and organize and bark into military precision. So, please, please, please listen to me, and let your creativity play in the field with all the butterflies and flowers for a long time, gathering Shimmering Images and writing them, gathering and writing.

Then, and only then, turn to the work of building a house from your material. The house, the architecture, is what you will ultimately need, but it requires of you a different kind of thinking, and if you have not first done the original creation, this part of the process can shut down that creation.

Structure is the central framework upon which you construct your tale. Without structure all the fancy, elaborate, well-honed craft in the world won't be effective, because structure links directly to what the story is about, what you are trying to say, what I call the Heart of the Story. And since structure and meaning are directly linked, your meaning will not be clear until you have a structure.

How then do you get your head and heart around this conundrum called structure? It's like a puzzle. You can't get the structure until you know the meaning. You can't know the meaning until you clarify the structure. What's a writer to do?

And to top that off you have all this material, a whole life screaming at you: Me! Me!

Here is the place where many writers bog down. Big gray clouds float into the brain, and everything disintegrates into chaos. And there you are again, right back at the beginning: Where do I start this darn story?

You can see the story in your head, but suddenly getting it on paper is insurmountable. Truly, mowing the lawn, doing the laundry, working out, filing your nails all seem of key importance. Right now.

Okay. Let's break this down into manageable chunks. Let me

walk you through the process I use to get a handle on structure in a piece of memoir.

In the beginning, I never focus on structure. For me, to start with structure can be paralyzing. To build some castle right in the beginning into which my story must fit is a backward approach, because I discover what it is I have to say—the shape of my castle—as I tell the story, and only as I discover what it is I have to say will I then be able to see a plausible form for the telling of the story. Three turrets? No . . . just one.

I simply begin by writing. I let my Shimmering Images flow onto the page, all the while knowing in the back of my mind that I will need a structure but resisting some rock-solid thing into which my tale must squeeze itself. I keep writing the images, and stay open. Pretty soon I get an inkling of what is important to the tale, what absolutely must be told, the shape of the opening moment, where I want the story to go. The concept around which it all pivots dances before my eyes. I "get" it. When this happens, when this kind of understanding appears, I shift my attention by considering a few common structures. I try them on my material, rather like slipping a shirt over my head and gazing in the mirror: How's that fit? How's it look? Sometimes I take the shirt off and try another. It's the same with these standard structures. I share them with you to soothe your nattering self-editor, that permanent resident of the left brain, who clamors for knowledge: Where are you going? What are you doing in this memoir?

Know this: Should you choose one of these structures, it may not end up being the best structure in the end; it may not be the shirt you wear. And that has to do with the fact that a book evolves as you work on it. You the writer have to be willing to accommodate the growing awareness that comes with that evolution; you have to be willing to let the story tell itself, too.

Chronological Structure

With this structure you begin at the beginning and go to the end. You begin with the Mountaintop event after which everything was different, and you walk through the story of how you came to terms with that event, focusing on key moments that played into that coming to terms and ending with some larger awareness of what that event meant to you, some insight into how it changed your life.

Sounds simple. Sounds straightforward, right? Well, it is and it isn't. Certainly Chronological Structure gives you a way to get going, but ultimately as you work your way into this simple structure you will find the complexity in what appears to be simple. You will realize that not every step of the coming-to-terms process needs to be included. As a matter of fact, it should not be; your story would simply go on and on with a bunch of stuff that bores the reader and isn't pertinent.

How then do you figure out what's pertinent to the story?

Good question.

And with that question you find yourself right back at the beginning: needing to know the Heart of the Story (its central meaning or goal—what issue did that life-changing event force you to face?), because only when you know the Heart will you be able to see what pertains to that Heart and what is extra. Only then will you know what must be in the story and what must be cut out. It's like sculpting a piece of marble: Certain chunks belong there, and others must be chipped away because they do not serve the form that is emerging. Suddenly even chronology becomes complicated.

The "e" Structure

Why do I use that name? Because it's rather like writing the low-ercased letter *e*. You start in the middle, circle back around, and come to the end. With "e" Structure you start the story in the middle of a chronological layout of events, circle back to the be-ginning event (the Mountaintop event), and then move forward chronologically, jumping over the event you opened with—when you get to it—and plowing on toward the end, Shimmering Im-age after Shimmering Image.

The "e" Structure/Variation #1

This variation on the previous structure begins your memoir near the conclusion of a chronological layout of events, opening the story with some compelling Shimmering Image that sits on the verge of your coming to terms with your Mountaintop event. Then you circle back to the beginning (the Mountaintop event) and move forward through the chronological layout of Shimmer-ing Images, again jumping over the event you began with, and concluding the story.

Collage Structure

One really simple structure for a memoir involves lining up a bunch of Shimmering Images, giving each one a title naming the essence of the Shimmering Image, and then letting the collection of Images tell a larger story simply by being collected. That way you don't even have to write transitions between the separate Shimmering Images.

The trick with this kind of structure is that each of the Shimmering Images has to explore some shared larger topic—for example, your neighborhood, cousins, first job, pets—or they have to link in some subtle way thematically: Shimmering Images about parenting, traveling in Mexico, making an English garden . . . whatever. (And because it's memoir, the implied subtext is what parenting, traveling in Mexico, or making an English garden taught you about life and yourself.)

What happens with this collage approach is that the whole collection of little stories, their flow, and the unspoken but implied juxtapositions and connections within that flow take the readers to a place of greater understanding in the end. You don't have to tell readers what you want them to "get" about your life experience. You just show them a bunch of Shimmering Images, like a slide show of pictures.

As a writer, what I know about these structures is that while they may sound wonderfully simple—the perfect solution—and while they may satiate the control-seeking lobe of my brain, conceptual thinking of this sort rarely aligns with the process of creation.

I can hold this clear idea of a structure in my mind: "Oh, how cute . . . it's a little 'e,'" and then when I try to make the Shimmering Images fit that structure, they won't. They have a mind of their own. It's only after I've written a bunch of stuff and then considered template structures, moved around the Shimmering Images—like separate building blocks—mirroring and playing with those structures, that the right structure emerges, or that I realize: Hey, this is like a little "e."

What it comes down to is you simply have to let the material speak; you have to let it guide you. Yes, you steer, but you let it guide, too.

When you get to the structure stage of composition, you have to be willing to allow the two sides of your brain to dance together, sometimes being led by the logical, *I have a structure la di da* side and sometimes being guided by the *hey let's let this stuff float around and show me the meaning* side. That requires a leap of faith that unnerves many.

And I know that.

Regardless, I urge you forward in this process, because it works. Stay the course.

If you can get yourself to that place of self-trust where you are willing to consider one of the possible template structures presented here, hold it in your mind as you work, and yet also consider the possibility that the material itself may have guidance in it, not only will you have developed a trustworthy strategy for locating structure in memoir, but you also will have hurdled one of the biggest blocks a writer faces: trusting his creative self.

13

HEART OF THE STORY 101:

FINDING THE HIDDEN

MEANING

Let's sink more deeply into the process of unraveling struc-ture. Let's talk about Heart of the Story.

Any way you look at it—whether you choose one of the struc-tures from the last chapter or you choose to wing it—you will discover that to build a narrative structure, you still need two ba-sic things:

1. Story material to work with
2. Some idea of what that story material is exploring on a deeper level, a level that connects it to the lives of readers: Heart of the Story

This Heart will guide how you ultimately structure your memoir.

So, how do you find the Heart?

You begin by writing your pieces, your Shimmering Images, as I've instructed. Collect as many as you can that seem pertinent to the event you have chosen from your Mountaintop list and the Memory Map you have drawn. Write one Shimmering Image after another. Don't go back and polish. Keep writing. When you have a bunch of these images recorded, you begin to explore connections between them, you begin to ask, "What are they about?"

Even before you get to that question, though, you may discover that without your realizing it, the order in which you composed the Shimmering Images suggests a rough story line, and you may opt for Chronological Structure. As you work on shaping that chronology, lining up the Shimmering Images, you may discover there are minor narrative gaps between images; there are important stories missing. Those can be filled in once you have the key Shimmering Images lined up in a framework that feels right to you.

Still, to sculpt that final chronology—to know what to leave in and what to take out—you will need to identify the bigger idea the story is exploring, the Heart, the one central pulse that every element of the story must either directly or subtly hook into.

You'll still need the Heart of the Story.

Or say as you are writing Shimmering Images you discover internal connections between the material you hadn't seen when the images existed only in your mind. You may decide to rearrange the order of the images to reflect the connections you are finding in the stories. Maybe several of your Shimmering Images group around your grandmother, several around your mom, and several around your favorite place to hang out with friends. Maybe what you have is three separate memoirs exploring three potent parts of your life, or three sections of one memoir that can be put together with Collage Structure.

Heck, I don't know what creative synapses may fire for you once you start working with your Shimmering Images as building blocks. But what I do know is that you can't proclaim this structural stuff before you start writing the Shimmering Images. You have to let the recurrent memories present themselves in the quiet moments of your life, and you have to pay attention to those Shimmering Images. You have to really look into them to see what they tell you about your life.

When you pen the stories that are hiding in the images and then you write about the meaning that is hiding behind the images, you discover surprises about Heart of the Story. To find that hidden meaning you can ask some basic questions of your Shimmering Images:

- What emotional weight do they carry? How do they make you feel?
- Who are the people central to your images, without whom your story would collapse? Why are they important?
- Where is your story set? What about that location carries metaphorical meaning?

Answers to questions like these—probing self-exploratory queries—guide you behind the images and into Heart. When you ask these kinds of questions about a lot of Shimmering Images, you enter a world of layered meaning that exists behind the images. It is the essence of why they come back to you. Only by journeying into this labyrinthine place will you find the structure that will best serve your memoir.

This is nothing like deciding on a thesis statement for a high school research paper and proceeding in linear fashion. This is all about teasing the Muse to come out of the trees and dance with you around the fire of creation. And I can't tell you exactly how it works, because we are talking now about forces beyond the ken of ordinary folk. I can tell you, though, that if you let go and trust this process, it *will* grace you, just as it will your neighbor.

And I can tell you: It's a very cool process.

You can be as flexible as you need to be as you reel out your stories and hunt for the threads that connect them. Maybe you only have time to write one Shimmering Image every day. Maybe you write them in threes every other day. Maybe you get together with a writing buddy and write as many Shimmering Images as you can in two hours every Wednesday night. The trick—no matter how you go about creating the written material—is that you let your Shimmering Images be your building blocks, let them show you the way to a structure.

I can't say that enough: You don't impose a structure; you let the structure reveal itself.

As you write, you open yourself to the possibility there are secrets you don't even know yet. As you write, you open yourself to the possibility that you will discover something unseen behind the Shimmering Images, some notion, some heartstring that will launch you into greater awareness about what your collected memories really do mean.

14

HEART OF THE STORY 102:
UNLOCKING ONE WORD

Heart of the Story revolves around some human experience many people can identify with, not because they've lived your life but because they've had some parallel experience in their own life, like love or loss.

Heart of the Story is shared sensation around which the story pivots, an emotional pulse that connects your tale to the lives of your readers because it loops into the region of the universal.

You need to know this Heart, because in a memoir the reader enters the story with an expectation tapping its foot in the front of her brain: "Why am I reading this?" the expectation whines, hand on a hip. "What is it about?"

Whether you like it or not, readers have an eye-on-the-watch mentality. Subliminally the ticking question in their minds is: Why should I care? And they will be looking for an answer in the first few pages of your story.

It doesn't matter if you are writing a short or long memoir, you will need to get a grip on what the story is about to make it something readers will care about.

You will need to name its universal attributes, not on the page but in your writer's mind, so you can write at them.

What is the Mountaintop event that sets up your journey of discovery? What issue did it force you to face? Why do certain Shimmering Images keep coming back? What is the trail of those images revealing? What is the meaning behind those images?

Keep asking these questions.

You do not need to know the answers in the beginning. If you have written twenty-five Shimmering Images and you are only now glimpsing the Heart of the Story, I would say you are walking the path as you should.

Here are reminders for finding the Heart:

- Write a lot of Shimmering Images.
- Explore your Personal Archives.
- Do Larger World research.
- Go back to your Memory Map; see what new images rise; write those.
- Consider the structures talked about in the structure chapter.
- Move the Shimmering Images around, like pieces in a puzzle, looking for an "Aha!" moment of recognition. (Sometimes I write one word on a note card to symbolize each chapter, then put away the writing and simply move the cards around on a table, allowing my pattern-making mind to see connections my logical brain could never serve up.)

And all the while:

- Read widely.
- Listen to all kinds of music.

- Look at visual art.
- Wander the library or bookstore letting your curiosity explore.
- Get out into the natural world.
- Allow convergences and meaning to surface.
- Go back to all the Shimmering Images and ask yourself, "What are these about? What is it that is backing up my throat that I want to spit onto the page? What unspoken meaning has come over me?" And then you write about that.

Another way to get answers about the Heart of the Story is to share your collected Shimmering Images with a writing group. Don't spend time polishing the images. Read them to a trusted, honest, and wise group of writers who know your writing. Read them as the blazing Shimmering Images that sprang from your memory. Ask your fellow writers what connections they see between these images. What do they think the images are exploring? What issue, what concept, do the images all seem to huddle around? Is it home? Is it innocence? Are you looking at the meaning of discrimination, obsession, self-confidence, intimacy, faith?

Find one word. Name that larger something that seems to be throbbing—unbeknownst to you—beneath the tales. Let your writer friends name it.

Choose only one word.

Try the word on for size. Does it fit the essence of the coming-to-terms journey you went on after experiencing your Mountaintop event? If so, this may be the Heart of the Story.

Write about it. Put the word at the top of a sheet of paper and ponder in writing what that concept means to you. This kind of expansive reflection will become essential to the spinning out of your memoir.

Now you can take the Heart you've discovered and the Shimmering Images you've collected and build a house for your story. Now is the time to engage with structure.

If you know your story is about forgiveness, then every Shimmering Image you use has to link into that larger idea, advance it in some way, build on it. For example, if you are using Collage Structure and you are writing about your sisters and you discover the Heart you are exploring around them is forgiveness, then each Shimmering Image you tell readers has to show them a picture that in some way symbolizes, reflects, teaches, or just plain breaks their hearts over the idea of forgiveness. And it can't be done with finger-pointing and blame. If you find your stories headed in that direction, go back and read the chapters on compassion.

Instead, it must be done by finding in the memory the details that signify and develop the Heart and by using every writerly trick to highlight those details in subtle and tantalizing ways. Could forgiveness be shown to a sister by sitting by her bedside as she lay ill, even though the narrator hadn't seen her in three years? What details in that room—the sister's favorite garden flowers set in a vase on the bedside table perhaps?—could extend the Heart of forgiveness?

Could a Shimmering Image show three sisters alienated by misunderstanding laughing over ice cream, reunited finally, even though their personalities remain the same? Perhaps they chuckle as each realizes their cones are piled with childhood favorites, signifying how little they have changed. Could a scene like that, drawn with such details, hook into a Heart of forgiveness?

These are the kinds of elements you must seek in your memories, in your Shimmering Images, in the writing you craft, and when you do, you will end up on the doorstep of the universal, because these are the kinds of elements that parallel the lives of others. They define a story that makes a difference. And why write memoir if you don't want to give someone else a leg up by allowing him to witness your experience and what you learned?

As a writer you must understand the contract a story strikes with a reader, and you must get honest with yourself as a craftsperson about questions like these:

- How is the reader going to converge with my tale?
- How can I get her to feel her life through mine?

The answer is obviously through the Heart of the Story. But what does that require of you?

It requires that you navigate your story to a place that harbors universal emotions: love and hate, loss and fulfillment, fear and courage, joy and sorrow, trust and betrayal. In this place, the reader will bind his own experience with yours and his life will be changed as you, the hero of the story, find your way to its conclusion. So select Shimmering Images that reflect the Heart, and be honest for heaven's sakes; show us your vulnerability. If you do, you'll be coursing right along in the deep waters of universal emotions.

No, of course you don't set out to write of such things. You don't flop down at the kitchen table one morning and say, "I'm going to write about the small betrayals of life." But if you tell an honest story, if you are audacious and courageous with your material and your craft, if you work with patient inspection of yourself and generous understanding of others, if you are authentic in word and emotion, you will find your way to a place of knowing that automatically links your story to universal principles.

It is essential that you be patient with yourself as you enter this phase of the process. Finding the Heart can take time. Writing memoir is about much more than perfecting craft. It is about fine-tuning the self, because only from a place of personal clarity will you have access to the Heart of the Story, and only when you access that Heart will you find a structure that can best house it.

This, my friends, is hard work, but it is the core of what you must do as a memoirist, and it will net you riches.

PART III

The Tools to Craft
the Process

15

NARRATION AND REFLECTION

Once you've generated a lot of material, noodled around with it, and come to understand more clearly the Heart of the Story and the structure, you'll want to start thinking about the craft of writing, the tools you use to build your story.

Many of these tools you will have used already in your writing, without even thinking about them. As you hone your story, though, if there are sections that are not working, it will be easier to fix those sections if you understand what might be going wrong.

Two of the most basic tools the memoir writer uses are narration and reflection.

When you narrate, you tell a story; you relate a series of events. As a natural-born storyteller, you automatically know which event should come first, which next, and which you must hold till the end to get your listener to laugh or to stare, eyes bugged out, muttering, "Really?"

Think about the stories you tell your friends about your daily events—the silly interaction in the grocery store, the serendipitous meeting outside the health club, the close call on the freeway.

You narrate it all, placing each step of the story so it will carry the impact you want: funny or shocking.

The same thing holds true in the stringing together of a series of Shimmering Images. Each one has its internal narration, and the series itself has a kind of overarching narration—its own plausible unfolding. We call it Narrative Arc.

Reflection is what you do when you stop narrating the events, those heartbeat moments that transpired over time, and you begin pondering, hand on your chin, the scene you've described.

"Hmmm," you say to yourself. "What did that mean?"

And then you spin a few interpretations. Some fit better than others. You find the convergences and weave them into the "meaning making" that you are doing in your story. Imagine yourself as two people:

1. First you reel out a stretch of the story as you remember it happening—the color of the sky, the smell of your child's skin, the sound of the train in the distance, and what the woman standing next to you said that bright fall day.
2. Then you step back and think about that event from either the vantage point of the person you were then or the vantage point you occupy today. You set that Shimmering Image in a larger perspective; you ruminate on its meaning, dig around, and look for understanding.

As you reflect on your life, mixing in the deeper meaning of events, you may find that you cannot come to a perfect little box of understanding, tied up with a perfect little bow, all tidy and clear. Sometimes you find meaning that ties events together, and sometimes you don't. The reflective memoirist records all of this—yep, even the fact that sometimes you can't find meaning.

That is the honesty that will grab at the throat of your readers, the very thing that they, too, have encountered: that meaning in life often rises from the lack of simple answers. Meaning lies in the complexity, the mysteriousness, and the downright inexplicability of your adventures. To have the wherewithal to admit you can't make sense of it can be a great relief to a reader who can't make sense of certain things in her life, either. A chance to hear another person ponder that reality, out loud, is one of the gifts memoir can give.

All you have to do is turn to the audience, the reader, and say: "You know, I never did figure that out. . . ." And on you go with the tale. Memoir is not about having tidy answers for everything. It's about making a truth of your experience, and sometimes the truth is that you don't get it.

Using the tools of narration and reflection is another way to create character. To narrate a story and then lean back into a thoughtful pose and use reflection, you create a vivid image of the person who speaks, the narrator, you, our hero of the story. First you show that person in the scene (narrate). Then you give depth to the character by constructing meaning about that person and the event (reflect).

Even the ways in which you do the reflecting—the kind of language and the patterns of meaning making you choose for your story—reveal to your reader the character who is living the life. Do you use lots of metaphors and comparisons to the natural world? Do you look to Jungian psychology and world myths for your meaning, drawing comparisons between differing cultural beliefs? Do you find meaning in your faith and reflect that onto the page? Does your understanding of the world and your experience in it grow out of mothering four children? Do you use family dynamics as the source of your understanding in personal experience? Or perhaps you use the boardroom and the unspoken rules of business negotiations as a way to make sense of life. Whatever the locus of your perspective, its inherent qualities will teach the reader a great deal about the central character of the book.

But regardless of your individual slant on narration and reflection, the bottom line is always the same: When you narrate you are the storyteller standing before the campfire, a crowd of friends gathered round; you are telling them how some event unfolded: "First we went here, and then we did this, and then this happened, and then he said this. . . ." And on and on you go, holding them spellbound as you explain what transpired.

Reflection is that same speaker stretched out on the chaise lounge, cozy and warm, eyes on the distance, searching for the meaning in those events, chatting casually about what he sees and why he thinks he sees it. How did that happen? Why did it happen? And what did it mean? These are all perfect questions for the reflective writer to ponder.

In and out you go, narrating and reflecting, narrating and reflecting—one long woven chain of event and meaning. An entire memoir can be written using these two most basic skills.

It doesn't need to be any more complicated than that.

16

WHO ARE YOU?

When writing memoir you can mix together all sorts of tools. You can dance the narration/reflection samba of the last chapter from inside the character you were at the time the event happened—maybe you are writing about the summer you turned twenty-four and hitchhiked across America with your boyfriend. You may want to write from that girl's perspective, get inside her head, narrate and reflect on the story from that age and level of understanding. Or you can dance the narration/reflection samba from inside the person you are now, looking back at that summer, remembering it from a distance and writing about it from the perspective of the woman you are now.

Think about it.

Those two characters are different people. They swing their hips in different ways. The girl you were at twenty-four made sense of her life one way; the woman you are at fifty looks back and sees a different landscape.

So, my dear writer friend, the person you choose to be when you narrate and reflect can be played with, as just one more of your tools.

Imagine this: You write a Shimmering Image of when you were eight years old. The person you are when you speak on the page, whose head you are inside when you talk, could be the eight-year-old child. You'd choose words an eight-year-old uses. The meaning you would make would be that of an eight-year-old, however mature or immature that might be, but you stick with that person.

Or you could choose to tell the same story from the perspective of the person you are now, with all the vocabulary and insight and wisdom of your years. Samba—one-two-three.

Or you can mix it up. Sometimes you can be one, sometimes the other.

The choices are up to you.

The only rule I have about the whole shebang is that it has to work. What that means is the reader needs to stay in the "dream" of the story the entire time you are narrating and reflecting, dancing back and forth.

When readers come to a story, they want to be transported into an imaginary world. They are making a pact with the writer that goes something like this: If you tell me a story, I'll suspend my disbelief and go along with you. You need to keep me engaged in a seamless imaginary world. For that I will give you my attention, my heart, my soul, until the very last page.

Your part of the deal as the writer is to make sure you keep the reader engaged in a seamless story.

"Seamless" means there are no glitches, no slipups on the dance floor, no clomping on other people's feet causing them to wake up and scream, "Yikes! I'm not floating, I'm just another human being getting my feet trampled."

When you are narrating and you want to shift around from

one perspective—eight-year-old to adult, or whatever—you have to make the changes invisible, slipping and sliding into and out of voices and perceptions without revealing the craft.

Unless you are a natural or already quite practiced as a writer, some of this could get messy, and your reader could careen to a halt and bark, "Wait! A paragraph ago you were eight. Now you're sounding like a fifty-year-old. What's up?"

Your reader, with whom you made the sacred pact, has been tossed out of the dream. She puts down the book, picks up *USA Today*, clicks on the TV, does the laundry, and when she has time in her busy schedule, the book that gets picked up is not yours. Another gets piled right on top of it.

Dance over.

Often the solution is to choose one age to speak from and stay there. Maybe you narrate and reflect in your entire memoir—the scenes from when you were eight all the way up to fifty years old—with the insight and wisdom of the human you are right now.

Maybe you progress carefully, integrating in greater and greater wisdom as the hero ages through Shimmering Image after Shimmering Image.

Whatever method you develop for writing your story, you must know your dance steps. You must make conscious choices.

This is the kind of stuff you think about further down the path after you've written all those luscious Shimmering Images and begun to herd them into some kind of order. (Notice, this chapter comes near the end of the book, and I put it there for a reason. I don't want you worrying about this as you come out of the gate, when you should be generating material, letting the magic of memory weave your stories.)

Later, when you are shaping your Shimmering Images, smoothing them into a narrative that charts what happened after your Mountaintop event, that's when you start fooling around with craft tools. That's when you acknowledge that you've written some Shimmering Images from the child's viewpoint and some from the adult's.

That is when the editor in you steps forward and takes control.

17

WHERE ARE YOU SITTING?

I magine you are sitting at a table in a restaurant with your circle of girlfriends. It's lunchtime and you are celebrating Kate's birthday. You are laughing and telling secrets about your husband, work, your mother, whispering and lifting your eyebrows. Everyone around the room—you can feel it—is straining to hear a tidbit, because it all sounds juicy and delicious, and yet they can't quite nose their way in because you are keeping your voice just low enough for the table. Still, all that huddling together and whispering, the public privacy of it, can't help but attract attention. There is an air of mystery around your corner of the room.

That is a different way of speaking than if you were seated on a knoll outside your town addressing the populate over a loudspeaker: "Good citizens of MiddlesBurb, I have gathered you here today to tell you stories about my life in this fine village over the last forty years. I will begin with the time I fell in the river behind the cannery on Tweedledum Creek . . . blah-blah-blah. . . ."

It's all a matter of where you sit. Are you tucked in close to the group—chairs scraping together—murmuring in your listeners' ears, or posed elegantly in a Louis XV armchair, gazing over the valley and announcing for public consumption the goods of your life?

This choice will affect the words you use and the way the reader reacts to those words. Is the reader being given a secret or receiving, along with a burgeoning crowd, a more general reminiscence?

Will you, the speaker in the story, be intimate and personal with your reader, or will you be distant and formal with your language, the information you share, and the way you handle that information?

The voice you use for each is a world apart; the tone, the choice of language, and the emotions created are two separate communities of thought and feeling.

In the first the listener leans in, curious, expectant, waiting to hear some private moment. In the second the listener sits back and absorbs information, watching and considering, hearing some of what is said, skipping some, because it's interesting but not an intimate tidbit.

Both are useful forms of communication; neither is better than the other; both can be employed for advantage.

The question becomes: Which will best serve your story?

Imagine you are using the voice of that twenty-four-year-old girl you once were, hitchhiking the roads of America. She has some tales to tell—about that damned, and beloved, boyfriend of hers. She's going to whisper in the reader's ear, tell some secrets, suck that reader down inside her world, let that reader sit on her shoulder and hear her thoughts. She's going to be the twenty-four-year-old, stay in that mind and body, no deviations, and she is going to talk to that reader like a girlfriend.

But maybe that twenty-four-year-old is more interested in the towns they passed through and the characters they met along the road. Maybe the voice of our hitchhiking protagonist reports about the communities tucked into the West Virginia hills and the drivers who gave them rides. Maybe she chooses to share those details in a more formal voice, more distanced, more like the writer positioned on the knoll outside MiddlesBurb.

Or maybe the narrator uses both voices at different places in the book. Back and forth she goes, whispering in the ear, using the loudspeaker.

You can do the same. This is simply one more piece of craft you can manipulate.

Ask yourself: Where do I want to sit when I tell my story? What relationship will I have with my reader? Intimate? Formal?

To make things easy, you can stay put in one place and speak from there throughout the whole memoir. It doesn't have to be more complex than that.

If you do choose to play with both, speaking intimately and more formally in the same memoir, you will need to have a plan for managing the shifts in seating, or the shifts in perspective, we might say.

Will every other chapter be related from a different location—shoulder, knoll, shoulder, knoll?

Will there be separate sections within chapters in which the narrator speaks intimately and then more formally?

Whatever you decide, remember you do not want to throw your reader out of the dream of your story, so you'll need to control the back-and-forth, the moving in toward an intimate tone and out to a more formal one. Skipping around in the same paragraph could get confusing.

If you are up close and personal, be sure the words you use are up close and personal. When you move back, control the

sound of the voice. But most of all, be sure the transitions between the two are seamless.

Let's imagine that twenty-four-year-old girl narrating her
hitchhiking tale. Imagine her sitting at a restaurant table, whispering and laughing with friends. She might sound like this:

Well, let me tell you, that time we were in Appalachia and
those fellows clattered down the road in that pickup truck, and
Don, he stepped in front of me to shield me, you might say. I
felt like I'd walked into some kind of movie. I mean, it was like
a period piece—1942—with their tired work clothes and dusty
hats and the way they leaned their heads out the window at us,
those boys looking past Don and right at me. You should have
seen that boy in the middle. I thought he'd climb right over his
cousin to get his face clear of that boy's floppy hat. And there
was Don jockeying around in front of me, shifting with the
truck as it rumbled by, trying to block their view, but doing no
good. I appreciated it and all. He'd been such a jerk for so
many miles, goading me whenever we discussed Jimmy Carter
and his Presidency, or Sartre, or hell! what type of dog food to
feed Sally, our Australian shepherd who trotted out ahead of us
across America. It was nice to know he cared about me, I won't
deny that, but the stares of those men, they penetrated everything around us, and it wouldn't have mattered one bit that his
wiry body shielded mine if those boys had decided to stop.
Why, it was so unnerving, I forgot about the moody road, and
the shadowy hills, and the thirst that parched my throat.

But what if the narrator were more distant and formal in her
approach to the same memory. Someone addressing the good citizens of MiddlesBurb might sound like this:

When we entered West Virginia I became uncomfortable. Hitchhiking was not accepted there. We got few rides. Most people slowed to stare at us. One time, the man I was traveling with and I were on our way to a store a quarter mile from the main highway. I remember the land around us as nurturing—the intimacy of the mountains, the jumble of trees and undergrowth cascading into the valley—and yet the sky was so close the scene felt claustrophobic. An old farm truck came up behind us. I could see the store ahead at an intersection. There was a dirt parking lot in front. As the truck drew closer, I heard the engine gear down. At that moment my companion reached out and folded me behind him on the edge of the road. I looked up to see three men leering out the window of the Ford. I felt my friend's body stiffen; the pickup didn't stop, but when it pulled in at the store, we reversed our direction and retraced our steps back to the highway. My friend said we could find something to drink at the next town.

Obviously, these two voices are different. In the first, the girl is front and center. Her idiosyncratic voice guides the reader to lean in and cock an ear toward the narrator. In the second, the girl's voice is reeled in. The person speaking to us is more like a travel writer reporting the sights and sounds, her personality tucked in the background through language and phrasing choices.

Now, let's mix it up and see what happens when we put the two together:

Well, let me tell you, that time we were in Appalachia and those fellows clattered down the road in that pickup truck, and Don, he stepped in front of me to shield me, you might say. I felt like I'd walked into some kind of movie. I mean, it was like a period piece—1942—with their tired work clothes and dusty hats and the way they leaned their heads out the window at us, those boys looking past Don and right at me. I remember the land around us as nurturing—the intimacy of the mountains, the jumble of trees and undergrowth cascading into the valley—and yet the sky was so close the scene felt claustrophobic. And there was Don jockeying around in front of me, shifting with the truck as it rumbled by, trying to block their view, but doing no good. I appreciated it and all. He'd been such a jerk for so many miles, goading me whenever we discussed Jimmy Carter and his Presidency, or Sartre, or hell! what type of dog food to feed Sally, our Australian shepherd who trotted out ahead of us across America. I felt my friend's body stiffen; the pickup didn't stop, but when it pulled in at the store, we reversed our direction and traced our steps back to the highway. My friend said we could find something to drink at the next town.

Do you see the way the voice shifts around in this last example? First the voice is intimate and personal. Then that voice pulls back; language choices change. Colloquialisms evaporate. Verbs lose their color and juice. Then—bang!—the intimacy is back. Then—boom!—it's gone again. It's like reading two different people, a split personality right before our eyes.

Here's what I see happening in the battle over where the narrator is sitting, tucked in close to the restaurant table with her girlfriends or stiffly ensconced in a Louis XV chair on the knoll outside MiddlesBurb. I'll break it down so we are all in the same little boat, traversing together the ocean of memoir. Here the intimate voice is in bold.

Well, let me tell you, that time we were in Appalachia and those fellows clattered down the road in that pickup truck, and Don, he stepped in front of me to shield me, you might say. I felt like I'd walked into some kind of movie. I mean, it was like a period piece—1942—with their tired work clothes and dusty hats and the way they leaned their heads out the window at us, those boys looking past Don and right at me. I remember the land around us as nurturing—the intimacy of the mountains, the jumble of trees and undergrowth cascading into the valley—and yet the sky was so close the scene felt claustrophobic. **And there was Don jockeying around in front of me, shifting with the truck as it rumbled by, trying to block their view, but doing no good. I appreciated it and all. He'd been such a jerk for so many miles, goading me whenever we discussed Jimmy Carter and his Presidency, or Sartre, or hell! what type of dog food to feed Sally, our Australian shepherd who trotted out ahead of us across America.** I felt my friend's body stiffen; the pickup didn't stop, but when it pulled in at the store, we reversed our direction and retraced our steps back to the highway. My friend said we could find something to drink at the next town.

That kind of musical chairs—moving back and forth between different ways of speaking—right in the center of the same piece of writing is what you want to be careful about. You may have to really listen to your writing to determine if you are doing this. Read your material out loud to yourself, and tune in to the voice you hear speaking. Pay attention. Analyze your choices in vocabulary and sentence structure. Once you get the hang of this, you'll see how you can manipulate this aspect of craft, and ultimately you may even see how tools like this are fun to play with.

They make your stories more complex. And it is true, they also make your job as a memoirist more complex.

Just remember this: There is nothing wrong with going for the easy solution. You don't have to mess around with the tools presented in the last two chapters, but somewhere along your path as a writer you may become more interested in the craft. Then, you'll have these chapters.

18

MAKING A SCENE

The best way to bring your characters to life in your memoir is to borrow a tool of the fiction writer and make a scene, getting your characters talking back and forth and moving around in space and time. Think of it like a movie.

You look up at the screen of your memory and see yourself standing in the bedroom you shared with your sister trying on clothes, shouldering each other for space in front of the narrow mirror. You record on paper the key elements of that movement and dialogue, the perfect snippet that captures your sister's personality, the critical actions that carry the scene forward.

Or if your drunken carousing father comes in singing a Broadway tune, picks a fight with your brother over the location of the car outside the house, then passes out at the kitchen table with a smile on his face, your readers will learn a whole lot about who he was and the life you lived without your explanation. They get to see it. They get to watch the same mental images you see in your mind's eye.

When making a scene you don't have to show readers every movement of the characters. You don't have to show you and your sister walking into the room and getting the clothing out of the closet and drawers. You simply drop into the scene as the two girls jockey for space in front of the mirror, slipping in and out of blouses, sweaters, and skirts they snatch from each other's side of the closet. Choose only those actions that are most emblematic of the scene's purpose.

Perhaps your father's scene begins with his bellowing voice snaking through the kitchen window and filling the room with song. In the next moment he is in the room grasping the back of a kitchen chair, adding a tap dance flourish to the end of the song, just as he turns to your brother. You don't have to follow his every step up the sidewalk, the key in the lock.

Each scene is meant to show something specific, like the love you shared with your sister, despite the bickering. The dailiness of your life together, the normality of it all. Perhaps that sits in contrast to something that happens later in the memoir where you and your sister don't have contact anymore. She betrayed you in some small but significant way. Yet once upon a time you were the closest of friends.

Or perhaps the scene simply illustrates the complexity of your father's personality—his problems with alcohol, his love of music, his harsh judgment, and his simple bliss rolled into one.

As you pull together your Shimmering Images, you can mix scenes with the passages of narration and reflection or you can use mostly scenes, composing your memoir more like fiction— scene moving to scene with minimal narration in between. It's all possible today. Memoirs come in all shapes and sizes, and no one way is better than another.

Listen to your natural voice. Are you more comfortable narrating from a distance, sitting on that knoll telling us what happened and then musing about what it all meant? Or do you like to be right there eyeball-to-eyeball with friends and family members, reliving it like an actor on the stage? What comes most easily to your fingers as they hit the keyboard? What flows automatically out of your pen when you write longhand?

Let the Shimmering Images be what they want to be. If they come out as scenes, great. If they come out as narration and reflection, great. Just let them be what you naturally record. Later, if you want to rewrite a certain Shimmering Image that came out as narration and reflection and turn it into a scene, add a few lines of dialogue, go for it. Or maybe you want to add some narration, condense a series of scenes. Give it a try. Summarize. Then lean back in your writer's chaise lounge, gaze through the smoke of time, and muse on the meaning of those summarized scenes. Integrate in your new impressions.

The bottom line with any of these techniques is that whatever tools you use to compose the story, they must be made, in the end, to fit together seamlessly. There can be no clunky transitions between scenes with dialogue and narration with reflection.

Sometimes the easiest way to do this is to divide the different tools into different chapters. In chapter 1 you narrate and reflect. Chapter 2 is a scene. Chapter 3 comprises narrating and reflecting. And on and on. This is a grossly simplified approach, but you get the idea. When you divide things up in an organized way it signals to the reader that there is a natural order to the shifts. The reader's mind is then geared to accept the transitions. Whatever pattern you devise, it must make sense to the reading mind.

All of this craft, whatever approach you choose, is directed toward making meaning. That's why we write memoir, to make meaning of our lives. Life when we are living it feels like a series of random events. "There is no pattern," you say, or, "Why are these things happening? What do they mean? Why me?"

When you write memoir and narrate and reflect, or put yourself and your compatriots into a shared scene and play out the action, you are using the various tools of the writer to order the random events.

Stories order chaos and make sense of our lives. In the process, the story has a magical way of answering old questions and transforming random events into meaning you can carry into the future with grace.

19

WORDS LIKE PAINTINGS

Most of us have heard of metaphors. Some of us have heard of and can define the simile. But that's the kind of literary mumbo jumbo I promised I wouldn't bury you with in this handy little guide to writing memoir. What I'm going to do in this chapter, then, is lump them together and talk about what they can do for your writing under one heading: imagery.

Imagery is another writerly tool, a game we play with language, where we take two things that are very different and we say they are like each other. The resulting collision produces a picture as rich as a canvas of oils in the reader's mind.

When we create these kinds of pictures, we can either use the word "like" or not. For example: frowns like bent nails.

Referring to birds, I might say: "Arrows in the afternoon sky."

Either way you write it, the goal is to compare two unlike things and through that comparison stimulate in the reader an awareness bigger, more beautiful, and more meaningful than either separate image can create. We expand the power of our words when we use imagery.

Imagery of this sort may come easily to you, or it may not.

Whatever your comfort level with imagery, I'm going to teach you a little exercise I devised for myself that you can do any old time—while commuting, washing the dishes, walking the golf course—and increase your comfort level with this writerly tool. Whenever you have time to let your mind wander is a good time to practice making images with words.

When I was teaching myself how to write a book, I made imagery naturally, but I didn't understand how to beckon language imagery on demand. Sure, I understood the definition of a metaphor, but nobody actually gave me a way to create one. When I was writing my book, *Hawk Flies Above,* and when I wrote the "Notebooks" that separated chapters, I watched what I did to create a union between two chapters.

The "Notebooks" are individual entries, each named after and focused on some aspect of the natural world—"Cottonwoods," "Dragonflies," "Hawks." There are twelve "Notebooks" in *Hawk Flies Above,* and I found as I wrote them that they functioned as metaphors joining the two chapters. Not only was I sharing basic information in each "Notebook" about a tree, insect, or bird, but I was also seeking convergences between the content at the end of one chapter and the content at the beginning of the next. That process, I came to recognize later, was exactly the process one uses to conjure imagery.

Try this:

1. Place in your mind one concrete thing you want to play with, like birds, or a frown, or your pet iguana when it is sleeping. Get a picture of that thing up on the screen of your imagination. Let's call it screen #1. Let it float there, like a movie still. Look at it. Observe its qualities. Observe its movement, color, nature.

2. One by one, let other objects come to mind and float onto another mental screen, screen #2, right alongside the first image. You now have two simultaneous movie screens in your mind, each holding an image of a thing.

3. Ask yourself whether you see anything similar between the two things, some element of their separateness that feels analogous. You don't need to be able to analyze it in some literary way. Simply look at the pictures and follow what your intuition tells you.

For me a bird tossing itself through the air on a sunny summer day looks like an arrow arcing through the sky. That arrow appears when I look at the bird in my mind—they fly fast and straight like little projectiles. In other words, I place an image of a compact finch throwing itself forward on screen #1 and wait to see what appears on screen #2. The arrow shows up, and I like the way the two things go together. I get a bigger image from the two than I would by just saying "a bird flying."

This whole screen #1/screen #2 thing is a place of experimentation. For example, let's try some images that don't work. Okay, we're holding the picture of the bird, wings tucked tight to its body heaving itself through the air, pumping, then heaving, pumping, heaving, and, let's see, conjure up an image of a dump truck. Hmmm . . . nope. Nothing about those two pictures goes together for me. Or how 'bout a chocolate-chip cookie . . . hmmm. . . . There's the little bird on screen #1, and there's the cookie on screen #2. Nope. Doesn't work for me.

How do I beckon the images that work?

I throw that first image up onto the screen. I let it sit there, and then I let my mind go quiet. I let whatever might like to parade onto screen #2 march right through, but all the time I'm looking at that first image and I'm asking in the back of my mind: What is it like? What is it like? A bird flying is like a chocolate-chip cookie . . . a bird flying is like an arrow. . . .

I hold steady and quiet in that inner realm, and I allow whatever wants to shimmy onto screen #2 to come on up and audition. All I have to do is look at the two images as they stand side by side and make up my mind: Yes. No.

When I find a unison I like, which seems to carry some weight, some meaning bigger than "bird flying," I go with it. I put it in the sentence. Later, as I rewrite and rewrite, I'll revisit that image a million times, and I will know in my bones if it works.

Okay, I admit, some of this screen #1/screen #2 stuff is native talent, but I know you all can throw little pictures onto your viewing screens, and I know you can look at them and you can make decisions. It's no different from letting the Shimmering Images rise and then recording what you see.

I've grown much better at this over the years, especially since I took the time to figure out how I made these kinds of literary images. Now I know a lot of it is practice. You can get better, too.

So, let's do another.

One day when I was perusing old family photos I came across some shots of my grandfather William Norton and his sister Evelyn Norton outside a country schoolhouse on the plains of dirt-poor southeastern Nebraska in the early 1900s. It was a grim photo. The eyes of those first-generation Swedish immigrants looked old. Some of the children had no shoes. Their clothes were too small and worn thin. No one smiled, but my great-aunt and grandfather seemed particularly serious. I stared for the longest time trying to get inside their skin. How would I describe them? Their tight faces floated into my viewing room, hovered on the screen. I saw again the hard eyes, the downturned corners of narrow lips . . . and onto screen #2 floated an image of a nail, all rusty and bent, and there it was: frowns like bent nails.

Of course frowns are not nails, but something about nails left out in the rain, abandoned and spent, resonated for me with the lives those children must have lived, shown to me through eyes too old for their years, and the sad shape of their mouths.

When I write "frowns like bent nails," I say much more to my reader than I do with the words "they frowned" or "they were not smiling." I imply a whole world with that image of the discarded nail, a whole world that I then do not have to talk about.

And that is one of the gifts of imagery; besides bringing beauty to your writing, it brings metaphoric weight of meaning.

That's why imagery needs to fit. The dump truck was wrong; the chocolate-chip cookie was wrong. Neither added the kind of background meaning that would enhance the story, although we might have played with those comparisons and come up with something wonderfully silly.

This playing with imagery is something to do once the story is in place, once the arc of the narrative has crystalized and you have the freedom to go back and toy with lines.

Playing with metaphors is something to do on a summer evening when you kick through gravel on the park road, glancing at the peach-colored sky, sun setting slowly into the dome of earth. Imagery comes when we allow our image-making minds to relax into the possibilities of unlikely comparisons, when we don't force them, when we allow the impossible to become possible.

To practice summoning up images makes the likelihood of

their appearance in your writing life more sure, and it makes your comfort level using them skyrocket.

I like to stare at the summer sky on days when the heat soaks my bones and allow the clouds to seep into shapes that imply all notions of critters. When I get to that space of imagination, I know I am in the land of imagery.

20

THE CLICHÉ TRAP

Question: What is a cliché?

Answer: A tried-and-true phrase that has been said over and over and beaten to a pulp by its repetition.

Hmmm . . . this response is a bit like those drawings in the *Highlights* magazines I read as a kid. There was a black-and-white drawing in every issue in which were hidden a number of objects, drawn into the lines of the image, which the reader had to locate.

Well, where are the clichés in the preceding definition?

1. Tried-and-true
2. Beaten to a pulp

We have heard these phrases so many times that they cease to carry any originality. They are like stock characters in a novel—nothing surprising sets them apart from any of the other characters. Clichés fill the gap between nouns and verbs, like junk food between lunch and dinner. They take up space but offer little.

They relieve writers from doing any work.

They make for sleepy sentences.

Here are some more clichés:

- Nose to the grindstone
- Piece of cake
- Been there, done that
- Vicious circle
- No laughing matter
- You could have heard a pin drop
- Like a duck to water
- Never a dull moment
- Straw that broke the camel's back
- Knight in shining armor
- First and foremost
- Cross to bear
- Keep me posted
- Wrong side of the bed
- Leap of faith
- Sob story
- Enough is enough
- Business as usual

The list goes on and on. Yikes! Even the phrase "the list goes on and on" is a cliché, or what I call "falling-asleep writing." I could have written instead: "There are dozens of examples yapping for space in this chapter."

Always watch in your writing for that phrase that slips out too easily, that rings in the ear with familiarity. It may feel clever and comfortable. It may seem to say exactly what you want to say. Chances are if it does, it's a cliché.

What can you do to avoid filling your prose with clichés? Sometimes you go ahead and write them, because the cliché offers a shortcut for expression. You can, first, get out the raw thought or feeling that needs to occupy space in your memoir. But later you must go back and rewrite it; you must find a more complex way to bring life to the moment you lived.

In fiction there may actually be a character who speaks in clichés. I can imagine creating such a person whose personality hinges on trite language. It could work.

In memoir, it doesn't, because in memoir it's all about voice. "Who is that incredible soul speaking to us through the story?" we ask. We want to read on in memoir because the voice of the narrator is fresh, and real, and honest, and full of integrity, and like no other voice we have witnessed. Clichés will rob you of the ability to create that voice.

This is how I deal with clichés:

1. I go ahead and write them in the first draft, if I need to, for expediency, to get onto a key and ephemeral idea or memory slip-sliding its way out of reach. I go ahead and plug in the cliché, knowing I will have to come back to it.

2. Once the draft of the chapter or story is done, I go back and read the entire sentence that contains the cliché, maybe even the paragraph or page, and I ask myself, "What are you trying to say?"

3. I make myself pause at that moment and think about it. I stay right there, pondering, working on an answer—what am I trying to say? . . . what am I trying to say?—until I can articulate my thoughts.

4. Once I understand myself, I find a fresh way to deliver the

essence of my message. I use new words. I get to the heart of what I am trying to communicate and find a truly "Lisa" way to say it.

Sometimes the essence of my message is the stumbling answer that issues forth when I keep hammering myself with the question: "What are you trying to say?" I go ahead and stumble it onto the page, and then I craft it. That is the work of a writer.

Rewriting clichés takes effort, but if you want to create a voice that is your own in your memoir, you will take the time to consider the clichés you have written and make conscious choices about whether to keep them or find new words. When you do this, when you engage with the craft of writing in this way, you stand in the heart of story making. It's a great place to be, because when you are poised in that singular breath of language, art, meaning, and expression you are a writer. Welcome to the club.

THE LAST WORD

Dear Reader,

I'm happy you made it to that last sentence and to "the club." The fact that you're here tells me you feel driven to write a story about your life that will transform it, a story that will entertain readers and give them doorways to transform their own lives. That willingness tells me you have a big spirit. Why? Because this is hard work, and I know it. The full circle of writing memoir is more than conjuring Shimmering Images, engaging in Mountaintop exercises, drawing Memory Maps, exploring Personal Archives, or looking for the Heart of the Story. It is more than writing draft after draft seeking Larger World connections and elusive, mythic patterns that will link your separate images into a transformative whole. It is more than learning and practicing tools, like imagery and the eradication of clichés.

It is about learning and practicing the self.

And I am in awe when I witness that. Awe is next to godliness, so thank you for letting me witness it in you and brush up against the divine.

Many of you, no doubt, are itching to get to the next step, or what you think is the next step: publishing. But this is not a book about the process of getting published. This is a handy little guide to writing memoir. I am not as concerned with publishing as I am with the act of creating a new story by which you can live your life—and that is exactly what writing memoir is all about. It's the act of ordering the chaos of the past, assigning meaning through the narrative process, and simultaneously creating a truth you can carry into the future, upon which you can base future choices—like what you will say in your mind and tell other people you deserve and can achieve. All such potentialities rise out of the story you make of your life experiences. That act of storytelling is mythmaking. Writing memoir is storytelling; whatever myth you sculpt from your past will influence your future.

That's what matters to me, because you are creating for yourself a new paradigm, a new way of being in the world, and that can shake things up. That audacious act has within it the seeds of change, and if you'll remember, those were some of my first words, at the beginning of this book, about why I do this work. I want to give you the tools to change your life and through that process to change the lives of others.

These things I can say:

- Selling a book to a New York publisher is hard work.
- Many writers are finding publishing outlets through smaller presses.
- Many people will never publish a book.
- Many writers will happily self-publish.
- And some among you will get that dream contract.

You choose what is best for you. Just remember that the primary importance is making narrative. It is that journey, in the whole scope of this swirling planet and our minuscule lives upon it, that can make a real difference. In the face of all the chaos out there, you can sit down at your desk and make a truth; you can create art. That simple act will be the basis of your continued life as a writer and artist—not whether you do or do not publish a book.

The work itself—the crafting from life material a narrative that not only houses wisdom and laughter but also gives you access to the next project, the next story that will buoy your talent and curiosity until another quest for personal discovery begins—that is the bedrock of the memoirist's work.

You make a story, you change your life. That's transformation.

You write another memoir, you change your life again. That's evolution.

My greatest hope is that you will stick with these tools and techniques until you have completed your memoir. There is only one path to the dream of a book, and it is through the chaos of creation. Over and over you can return to this guide and the process it shares, mining your memory and crafting Shimmering Images. These ideas will not become less useful with the passage of time. You will become more sophisticated, but these simple techniques will endure as a foundation for the exploration of your life through memoir.

I hope you will use them forever, and I hope someday I will meet you—whoever you may be—at a workshop or class I am teaching. I hope you will walk up to me and say, "Hi. My name is ———, and I read your book *Shimmering Images*." Journeying together in this way has made us friends, and why shouldn't friends greet each other when they meet?

As always, your friend and writing mentor,

Lisa Dale Norton
Santa Fe, New Mexico

ABOUT THE AUTHOR

Ray Bidegain

Lisa's book *Hawk Flies Above: Journey to the Heart of the Sandhills* has been compared to the writing of Annie Dillard and Terry Tempest Williams. A mixture of memoir and nature writing, *Hawk Flies Above* charts Lisa's return to her homeland, the Sandhills region of Nebraska, for healing. In the process, the story explores convergences between the landscape of soul and the landscape of the Sandhills, exposing environmental problems plaguing the Hills.

Lisa holds degrees from Reed College and the University of Iowa. She has been on the faculty of Augustana College and Pacific Lutheran University, has taught writing at numerous colleges and universities, and has appeared on television, radio, and before live audiences nationwide, speaking about her two passions: writing and the transformative power of story.

During the 1990s Lisa founded and directed Neahkahnie Institute on the coast of Oregon, which hosted writing workshops and the Onion Peak Reading Series. Currently she teaches creative nonfiction for the UCLA Extension Writers' Program, the granddaddy of extension programs in the United States; writes a monthly column for Authorlink.com, *Your Life as Story: Writing Narrative Nonfiction;* speaks and teaches around the country; and consults with clients on writing books. She lives in Santa Fe.

Workshops

Lisa is available to teach workshops based on *Shimmering Images: A Handy Little Guide to Writing Memoir.* She is an inspiring, supportive teacher who will have you laughing through your tears as you mine your memory for story and craft a compelling narrative from the gems you find. Three of her most popular workshops are:

Shimmering Images: A Handy Little Guide to Writing Memoir. In this workshop you learn how to weave an engaging personal story by anchoring it around key Shimmering Images. Lisa teaches you how to capture your most powerful memories, link them together, and focus on details that count. You leave the workshop with a completed short memoir and a technique to use over and over for writing other stories.

The Compassionate Memoir: Writing as Transformation. Everything is held together with stories. When you direct the stories you tell, you shape the course of your life. In this workshop, you learn how to push your Shimmering Images beyond personal events into a bigger story that moves readers' hearts and changes their lives. You do this by focusing on language and practicing how to write stories that rename what memories mean.

Structuring the Memoir: Finding Your Life's Narrative Arc. To the writer of memoir everything seems important. But compelling stories have narrative arcs that include some events and exclude others. If they do not, readers lose interest quickly. In this workshop, you learn what a narrative arc is, how to expand chronological memory into a layered storyline, and what it takes to keep readers engaged to the very last page.

Conference Addresses

Lisa inspires people. When she speaks about story and the power of narrative, listeners see how personal stories can change individual lives and, ultimately, the world. Whether speaking to an audience of writers, therapists, teachers, small business owners, students, or individuals seeking personal growth, Lisa gets people excited about writing or telling their stories in new and enlightened ways. She can kick off your event with a funny and informed talk about how the stories we tell shape the lives we lead. You don't need to be a writer to understand the simple wisdom of this formula.

Consulting

Lisa works with clients around the country on writing books. Her specialty is narrative nonfiction, which includes memoir, travel writing, the essay, and creative nonfiction. What these forms share is a storyline crafted from life material.

Lisa helps her clients clarify writing goals and complete book manuscripts. Writers consult with her on the nuances of story structure, narrative voice, character development, and the creative process, and receive coaching for the entire project, from concept generation through the bugaboo of supposed writer's block, the finer points of punctuation, and manuscript preparation.

For more information, or to hire Lisa for a workshop, to speak at conferences or events, or to discuss your book project with her, visit her Web site, at www.lisadalenorton.com.

You may contact Lisa Dale Norton through either of her Web sites,

www.lisadalenorton.com

or

www.shimmeringimages-book.com

or by writing to her c/o her publisher:

St. Martin's Press
175 Fifth Avenue
New York, NY 10010